Longships Lighthouse

(photo: Norman Fitkin)

TRINITY HOUSE
THE SUPER SILENT SERVICE

Michael Tarrant

First Impression—1998

ISBN 1 85902 469 6

Printed in Wales at
Gomer Press, Llandysul, Ceredigion

CONTENTS

Acknowledgements

My thanks are due to all those members of the Trinity House Service who sent letters and items of interest that I might be able to use in this book. Sadly, I was unable to use many of them and I hope none will be upset because a particular contribution has been omitted.

My thanks are also due to the Elder Brethren of Trinity House for their permission to trawl through some of their archives and other records, to Mr. Richard Gibson for permission to use the extensive Gibson collection, to Mr Norman Fitkin and many other individuals and publishers for other photographic material. There are instances where it has been impossible to trace or contact the copyright holder. The publishers apologise for this and, if notified, will be pleased to rectify any errors or omissions at the earliest opportunity.

I am particularly grateful to my friend and former colleague Richard Woodman for his permission to use items from his book *Keepers of the Sea*.

I hope I have written enough to show my readers some of the inside story of this most important maritime service. It is several centuries old, but was subject to subtle changes through most of them. These changes have accelerated in the past dozen years since my retirement and I can hardly recognise it now. I do not doubt it will continue through the next century and I wish it well.

Finally I am pleased to dedicate the book to my very dear wife with my love and my appreciation for her support while I was engaged in writing it.

BUCKINGHAM PALACE.

The seaman has always had to face two great challenges; how to find his way safely across the oceans and in coastal waters, and how to handle his ship in restricted estuaries and harbours.

Henry VIII attempted to solve both these problems when in 1514 he established 'The Guild Fraternity, or Brotherhood of the Most Glorious and Undivided Trinity in the Parish of Deptford Strond' - more usually known as the Corporation of Trinity House. The purpose was to provide aids to navigation in coastal waters and a pilotage service in the approaches to ports and harbours.

The King hit on a remarkably successful formula. It is an independent agency governed by a body of experienced seamen elected by seamen and it anticipated the principle of 'the user pays' by several centuries.

In recent years electronics and automation have transformed the activities of the Corporation and the old ways are inevitably dying out. The author of 'Super Silent Service' has recorded his wealth of experience just in time and I am sure that his book will become highly valued as a social history of a great maritime institution.

Philip

General aids to navigation maintained by Trinity House in England, Wales and the Channel Islands

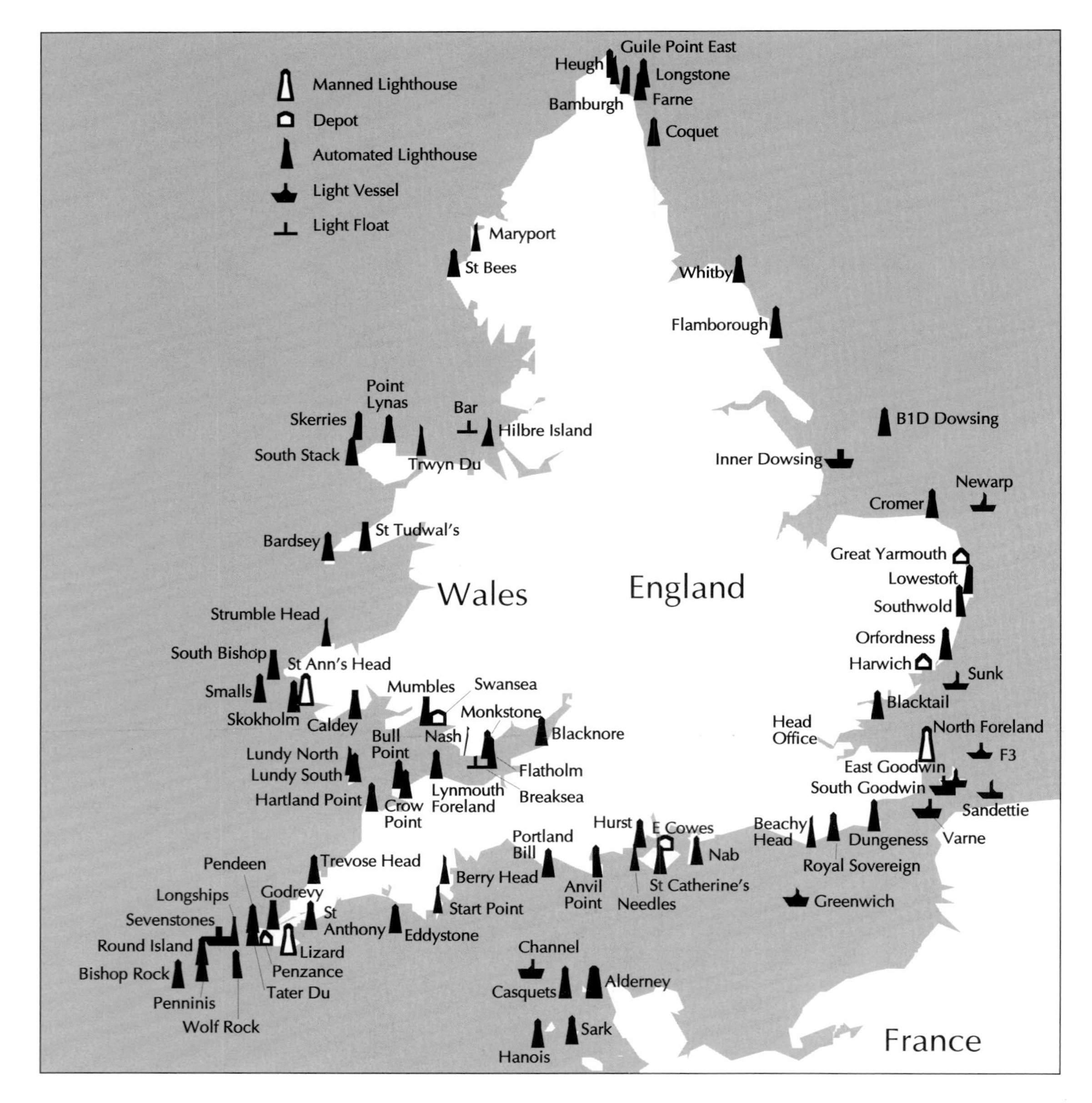

Preface

Extract from Trinity House Regulations :

> *'No official in the service of the Corporation shall contribute to the press, or supply to any journalist, or other person for publication material relating to the affairs of the Trinity House, except with the special sanction of the Board in every instance.'*
>
> *23rd October 1894*

No doubt the above regulation was instituted for very sound reasons but it certainly curtailed any news being spread abroad of the work performed by the ships and personnel in the Trinity House Service. Much of that enforced silence regarding the work has largely disappeared but prior to World War II the regulation had a very marked effect indeed. Hopefully this book will spread a little light on some of the lesser known activities and incidents of this important service.

Most people living in England and Wales are aware of the lighthouses, lightships and buoys which surround our coasts but comparatively few of them know how they are managed and by whom. It often comes as a great surprise when they learn that the work is done by a body known as the Corporation of Trinity House and not by either the Navy or the Coastguard Service. Trinity House is one of the oldest institutions in England, being able to trace its origin back to 1514 when King Henry the Eighth granted it a Charter for the management of pilots who brought ships into our ports and rivers.

He also gave it the title of 'The Guild, Fraternity, or Brotherhood of the Most Glorious and Undivided Trinity and of Saint Clement in the Parish of Deptford Strond', and gave control to the Master, Wardens and Assistants who are known as the Elder Brethren. There is also a group of Younger Brethren who are drawn from all walks of life unlike the Elder Brethren who are all seafarers.

Trinity Brethren apparently existed long before this although any written evidence for this has not survived. There are however two graves of Trinity Brethren in Leigh Church in Essex. The names are recorded as Richard Haddock, who died in 1453, and Robert Salmon, who died in 1471, and it is presumed that they belonged to the Society founded by King Alfred or Archbishop Langton to look after the welfare and safety of seamen when the Danes raided the east coast of England. This was the beginning of the pilotage service.

The first Act of Parliament to concern Trinity House came in 1566 during the reign of Queen Elizabeth the First and greatly increased their duties and responsibilities. This was well summed up by the phrase '. . . shall and may erect and set up . . . such and so many Beacons, Marks and Signs for the sea'. Thus the Lighthouse Service came into being and grew very slowly. First came the 'Beacons', just poles secured at prominent places in the mouth of rivers, then 'Marks' of various sorts, frequently just Church towers or wooden casks moored to mark a channel.

Then, much later, came the 'Signs' in the shape of lighthouses—first at Caister in Norfolk in 1600 and these slowly spread along the east, south and west coasts of England and Wales. Eventually the 'Signs for the sea' went fully afloat in the shape of lightships. The first one was at the Nore in the mouth of the Thames in 1732 and thereafter the proliferation of the buoyage system and the Service itself went from strength to strength.

All these establishments and of course the hundreds of buoys which eventually marked the channels, wrecks, shoals and isolated dangers around our shores needed a permanent fleet of ships to service them, and still do.

A painting by Thomas Whitcombe in 1788 of the Trinity Yacht passing Caskets (*sic*) Lighthouse. This station originally had 3 lights on separate towers as can be seen. All three are still there but only one now has a light. These three were installed long before flashing lights were invented, enabling sailing ships coming in from the Atlantic to distinguish between the single light on St. Mary's, Isles of Scilly, the two on the Lizard Point lighthouse and the three on Casquet's.

As with the other sections of the Trinity House Service this fleet began in a small way in the early 1600s and grew steadily. There have been almost 80 ships in the fleet since then and their story is very well documented in Richard Woodman's book *Keepers of the Sea.* Collectively they are known as 'the tenders'.

There have been many books devoted to the building of lighthouses and a few to the story of lightships but almost none to the story of life in the Trinity Service and what it involved. Much of this 'life' has already disappeared with modernisation. All the lightships are now automated and unmanned and so are the off-shore lighthouses. The shore stations will all be unmanned by the year 2000 and the fleet of Trinity House tenders is now reduced to two. This contraction of the world famous Trinity House Service is almost solely due to the new technology now available for operating the lights and of course to the new technology available to mariners, which reduces their need for Aids to Navigation around our coasts.

My purpose is to tell some of the story of this long era of the nautical history of England and Wales before the details are largely forgotten. There are scores of threads to be drawn together, memories to be revived and details dug out from various archives. My life in the Service covered 44 years from January 31st 1939, so I have a fair claim to be able to write such a story. It must inevitably contain much of my own personal history but I see no need to apologise on that score.

My own career, though a long and enjoyable one, did not provide experience of all the services provided by Trinity House. The important pilotage service, for instance, represented by the striking cover photograph, is one branch of the service whose history must be left for another to tell. The photograph featured is, of course, Trinity House Launch *Ready*, and the publishers apologise for referring to it incorrectly on the back cover as T.H.L. *Vectis*.

One of the archives I shall quote from at intervals is a list of 'Depot Ditties'. These were written by an old colleague, Commander C E K Kendal-Carpenter, who also spent a lifetime in the Service. All were composed many years before World War II and are interesting in their revelation of Service life 70 or 80 years ago. He died in November 1980 and I am grateful to his family for allowing me to collect a number of items from his library to use in this book.

TRINITY HOUSE FLAGS

The Master's Flag only flown on a ship if he is on board.

Flown by all Trinity House ships and Trinity House depots.

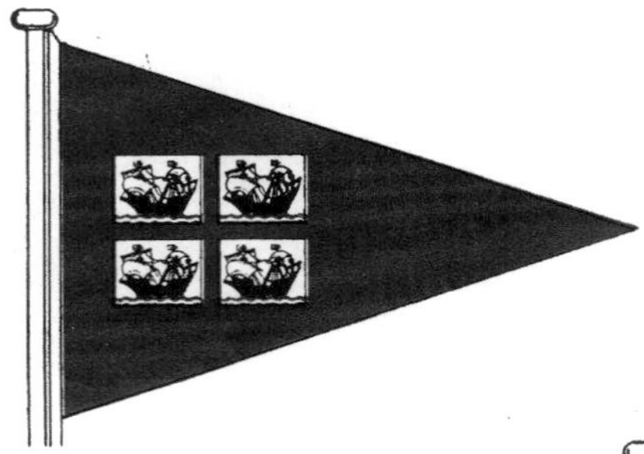

Flown on a tender if the District Superintendent is on board.

Only flown when the Deputy Master is on board.

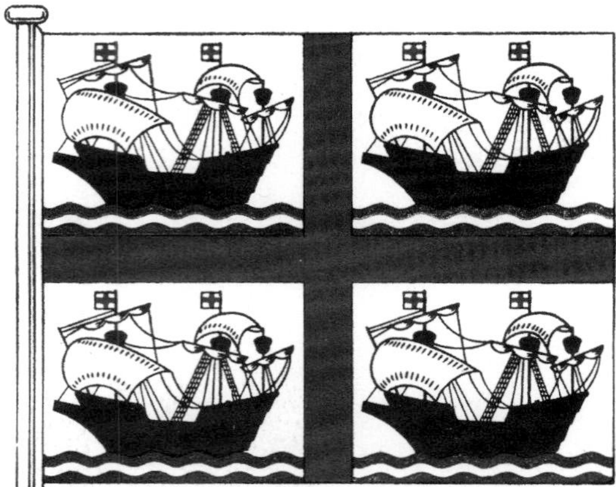

Flown on a tender if she has any Elder Brother on board.

Introduction

In the early days of the Trinity House Service its staff consisted of very isolated groups of personnel at various places around our coasts in the charge of local Agents and controlled from the headquarters of Trinity House in London. With the eventual expansion of floating seamarks from about 1700 onwards it was necessary to establish proper depots with facilities for preparing the buoys and lightvessels. These depots were only concerned with England and Wales which is still the limit of Trinity House Jurisdiction in the British Isles, and each one had a Lighthouse Tender attached to it to deal with the off-shore operations. These ships comprised the Trinity House Steam Vessel Service and their function was to attend on the Lightship Service, the Lighthouse Service and the buoy stations. All of these services are now known collectively as the Trinity House Lighthouse Service.

The personnel of these three Services were recruited separately since their duties and conditions of service were quite different. The various depots were each under the control of a District Superintendent after the post of Agent was abolished shortly before the turn of this century. The Superintendent usually lived in a house at the depot or else in the close vicinity. He was always promoted to that post after serving as Master of one of the Tenders. Part of his duties was to go afloat at intervals in one of the tenders to inspect the off-shore stations on his District.

The contraction of the Service mentioned earlier has included the abolition of the post of Superintendent and the depots are now supervised by an Officer-in-Charge who does not have sea-going experience as a rule.

When I joined the Service in 1939 the fleet of tenders comprised nine ships, and this number continued until 1970 when the first reduction of the fleet took place: it has continued steadily until now there are only the two tenders left to cover the whole of the English and Welsh coastline. Many changes happened in those 31 years from 1939 to 1970, including wartime losses and their necessary replacements. Trinity House suffered the loss of four ships during World War II and this will be documented in Chapter 9.

Although the limit of Trinity House's jurisdiction is still legally just the coast of England and Wales, their area of operation is now sometimes more extensive on occasions. There are two other Lighthouse Authorities in Britain—The Northern Lighthouse Board controls Scotland's coast and the Commissioners for Irish Lights look after Ireland's coast. However, the two authorities have to submit details of any buoyage schemes they propose to Trinity House.

Both of these bodies perform the same sort of work as Trinity House does and each has reduced its fleet of tenders as Trinity House has in recent years. As a consequence the ships of each of the three Authorities are always willing to help out the other Services if the need should arise. While acknowledging the importance of the two other authorities, I shall confine my attention in this book to the service I know best, namely that of Trinity House.

This Lightship Station was established in 1849 to mark a large Sandbank of the same name off the Norfolk Coast, withdrawn between the two Wars and permanently discontinued.

Relief work in the present day being carried out by helicopter, from a pad on the top of Bishop Rock Lighthouse, Isle of Scilly.

(photo: F. E. Gibson)

I hope to provide enough details of the various branches of the Service to give an insight into the work and life of the several thousands of men who lived and served through this era in Britain's nautical history. Otherwise all that long line of men and women who served in the Super Silent Service—as we called it—will be almost forgotten except by their descendants.

Hopefully this book will serve as a small testimonial to their skill and endurance and will recall some of the high-lights and low lights of that almost unknown life of service to the mariner, past and present.

Chapter 1

Personnel

The history of 'Trin', as it is called by most of its employees, is well documented elsewhere but one must dig very deep to find much detail of the life we led in serving the Honourable Corporation. A few people have hit the headlines for a brief moment and some have even been recorded for posterity as we shall see. In the main, though, the story is often one of considerable monotony and endless routine which is why no one has given very much attention to it. Indeed, the life was never meant to be anything else but endless, efficient routine. Men were picked for their reliability and skill but it was their dedication to the job which overcame that monotony and ensured they stayed the course until retirement. This was often after half a century of service to the Honourable Corporation, sometimes mispronounced as Horrible Corporation, but then nothing is perfect in this world!

Undoubtedly the most remarkable example of continuous long service must be that of the Knott family who were all lighthouse keepers. Their line began with William Knott, born in 1706 and who started work as a Keeper at South Foreland lighthouse in 1730 when it still used a coal fire as its light. He worked for 50 years until his death, when his son took over. The line of Knotts continued for a total of five generations of that name, nearly 200 years, and even after that for many more years, although not carrying the name of Knott. This was a result of a daughter marrying a keeper named Hall and subsequently the line continued into Grace Darling's family. The story has been written by a descendant, Elizabeth Roberts, in 1984 under the title *They All Lived in Lighthouses*.

This small army of men who gave such service to the mariner were not all keepers of lighthouses and lightships by any means. It included an equally loyal band of seamen who served in the fleet of tenders which ministered to their needs and an equally loyal and expert team of shore-based engineers—civil, mechanical, electrical and radio—with their attendant group of 'out station' workers in the field who dealt with the repair of defects and much of the manufacture and installation of new equipment.

Another large group, of men and women, attended to the considerable amount of clerical work in the Trinity House Depots around our coast and at the London Headquarters, Trinity House itself, at Tower Hill, London. They ordered stores, paid wages, arranged men and materials for all the stations in their various Districts, recruited new men for the Service as retirements came due and finally arranged for the pensions to be paid.

> The pen is mightier far than sword.
> (By executive men a fact deplored!)
> For nothing annoys a sailor more,
> Than *Immediate* memos from the shore.
>
> The career of the clerks, T.H.S,
> Is one of boredom—more or less.
> Altho' no doubt they get some thrills,
> Amongst their papers, Ink and quills.

This group of people are headed by the Secretary who is also a member of the Board although not an Elder Brother. One of his special duties was, and still is, to conduct the Swearing-in ceremony whenever a new Elder Brother is appointed. He is also a Civil Servant as are all the members of the clerical staff.

They are often regarded as a barrier between the Board and the 'afloat staff' although this is somewhat unkind since the Elder Brethren certainly need them to attend to all the records. They are also needed to advise the Board on all matters relevant to the efficient running of the whole Service. Occasional references in this book to messages and instructions received 'from on high' mostly emanate from this department.

The Courtroom at Trinity House, Tower Hill, London.

Everyone employed by Trinity House is subject to Civil Service rules and conditions and it is known as a Fringe Body of that organisation as a result. Much of this mundane work has long been forgotten with the advent of computers and new methods of compiling records. But glimpses of it can still be found in the memories of surviving personnel and very occasionally in notebooks and old records which have miraculously escaped destruction. There was a vast amount of these paper records at one time. Every lightship, every depot, every lighthouse, had to make monthly returns: personnel on duty, stores received and expended, hours worked, time spent on sounding for fog etc, etc. The tenders had similar returns to make about their work: stations attended (buoys, lighthouses, lightships), stores used and copies of their daily log books to be forwarded.

When I joined the Steam Vessel Service in 1939 there were literally tons and tons of these old records stored in basement archives at Trinity House London. Not that I ever saw them but their existence is recorded in Stanley Cooper's privately published account *Some Sidelights on Trinity House since 1921*. He tells how he and other junior staff in the 1920s had the task, once a year, of filing all these records in tunnel-like store-rooms beneath Trinity House. Although they were all neatly bundled and labelled he reveals that the final stage was to open the relevant door and just fling the bundles inside wherever a space could be found—never to be seen again. Stanley was another of those people who gave a lifetime of loyal service, eventually retiring as District Clerk at the Harwich depot in 1956.

I understand that one of his accomplishments was to persuade Trinity House to purchase a special accounting machine for the Workshops. This had not been contemplated previously but it dealt most efficiently with the mounds of paperwork which had to be handled there.

Those old records eventually proved to be wonderful fuel for the blaze started by incendiaries on the night of 29th December 1940 when that Headquarters building, Trinity House itself, was gutted. Presumably they had been accumulating since the previous fire which destroyed Trinity House in 1714. I doubt whether their loss was particularly noticed and it certainly was not mourned. It did not however prevent another similar accumulation after the war which led to the necessity for a vast clear-out of old records in 1989 when Trinity House underwent a complete refurbishment and updating.

One interesting old record which has survived is a Service List issued in 1910. This is a book which records the names and details of every man serving on the Lightships and Lighthouses in the Service on 1st April 1910 and all the Deck and Engine room Officers serving on the tenders also. It gives their date of birth and date of entry into the Service. In many cases it shows their dates of promotion and the stations they served at or the ships they sailed on. It contains 634 names of personnel and the earliest one recorded is W J Rees. He entered the Service in June 1865 and retired in March 1911 after serving at six different lighthouses.

Officers and men of Trinity House Yacht *Irene* and Trinity House Ship *Stella*. (Taken at Blackwall, prior to 1914).

Crew of Trinity House Ship *Siren* at Milford Haven in 1904, in the grand uniform of the period.

(photo: *The Western Telegraph*)

Many others gave similar periods of service both before and after the book was compiled and whose record is now lost forever. There would have been twice that number of ratings who served on the tenders in the same period and there may have been another book listing their names which has not survived.

The book is also an historical record of Trinity House stations and throws an interesting light on how the Service has always been subject to change. Careful study of the names of stations which were manned for any period between 1865 and 1910 shows there were 91 lighthouses and 55 lightships at the beginning of that period. But the index of manned stations at the back of the book shows only 74 lighthouses were still manned in 1910. This quite considerable reduction of manpower indicates that even 100 years ago Trinity House was actively engaged in pruning the service being given to shipping. Even the dreaded word 'redundant' is to be found against names as far back as the 1890s, although it seems that many of those men were re-engaged within a few months; probably due to a retirement, when a man known to have a good record would be quickly re-engaged.

This Service List is really just a short phase in the story of Service personnel because men were first employed by Trinity House to establish, and maintain, buoys on the East coast around 1607, some three hundred years earlier. (See *Keepers of the Sea* for details.) These could reasonably be considered as the first Trinity Service personnel, to be followed at intermittent times by others employed to man lighthouses, lightships and the tenders to support them. There may easily have been twice as many who served, and retired, during those three centuries than are recorded in the 1910 list. I do not doubt, either, that another 1,000 or more came and went between 1910 and the present time whose record is also lost for ever.

There were of course plenty of Elder and Younger Brethren, a succession of whom served Trinity House from its beginning in 1514 to the present time. Their story is well recorded by G G Harris and other writers, and one is hesitant to include them as Service personnel. Some of the most notable among their ranks and up to recent years are: Sir Thomas Spert, the first Master of Trinity House and formerly Captain of the *Mary Rose*; Sir William Penn, whose son was founder of

The Lighthouse keeper and his family outside their quarters at the old Lundy light, circa 1890.
(Photo from *A Lundy Album* by Myrtle Langham.)

Pennsylvania; Samuel Pepys of diary fame, twice Master of Trinity House and the man who can justly be called the 'father' of the British Navy for his work as Secretary of the Navy Board; William Pitt, statesman; the Duke of Wellington; Lord Palmerston; Gladstone; Disraeli; Sir Winston Churchill; they have all worn the uniform of an Elder Brother and some of them reached the status of Master of Trinity House as well. The present occupant of that exalted position is H R H the Duke of Edinburgh.

Another whose name is rarely mentioned but who is well authenticated in the records is Sir Henry Mainwaring. His association began in 1627 as an Elder Brother and he was twice elected Master before being expelled on the orders of Oliver Cromwell in November 1642. His early years before joining Trinity House are also well documented and we learn that he was a convicted pirate! A highly successful one, apparently. Working from a base in Algeria he had a fleet of seventy ships at one time and amassed a huge fortune. He was convicted of piracy in his absence but subsequently accepted a free pardon from James I in 1616 on condition he gave up piracy. He accepted this condition and came ashore to settle at Dover. There he became Lord Warden of the Cinque Ports and Member of Parliament for Dover. A few years later he became an Elder Brother and then Master of Trinity House.

This little vignette of English history sometimes evokes the response 'so what's new in Trinity?' but there is no evidence of him introducing piratical ways into the Service! I learned a verse of doggerel when I was a young Apprentice which began :

Oh Elder Brethren of Trinity Guild,
With pomp and iniquity equally filled . . .

but whether its origins are bound up with Sir Henry or not are long forgotten, as I too have long forgotten any additional lines of the scurrilous verse.

I am pleased to report here that there was a more complimentary couplet which ran :

'Deny ourselves and work for others'
is the creed of Elder Brothers.

As an offering of thanks for his pardon Mainwaring wrote a 'Discourse on Pirates' for the King which revealed many of their safe havens and secret watering places. No doubt he also served as the inspiration for a subsequent 'Expedition against Pirates' mounted by Trinity House which was very successful. Sir Henry also wrote *The Seaman's Dictionary*, one of the earliest attempts at an instruction manual for seafarers and still applicable to terms and words in common usage today. Before his death in 1658 he was considered 'the first and foremost seaman that England possessed'. His grave is at St Giles Church, Camberwell. The full story can be found in *Life and Works of Sir Henry Mainwaring* published by the Navy Records Society, vol.54 and 56, 1920/21.

Chapter 2

The Trinity House Workshops

I have already mentioned the highly important group of engineers and other workers who were shore based and attended to all the repair work needed to keep the lighthouses, lightships and buoys in good order over the years. Their base for nigh on two centuries was on the Thames at a depot at Blackwall in east London, except for a very few who were stationed at some of the other Trinity House depots. The shore staff existed quite amicably with the 'marine side' of the work at that depot which was in the charge of the Chief Superintendent until the blitz on London began.

Originally, in the early 1800s, the Blackwall depot was created simply as a place from which to conduct the reliefs of the lightships in the Thames Estuary and to attend to the increasing amount of buoy work in the same area. Trinity House first leased the site in 1803 from John and William Wells for this purpose and purchased it in 1815.

At that period of the Service's existence if any repair work was needed to any of the stations around the coast, buoys, lighthouses or lightships, this was arranged by the local Agent. As this work increased when Trinity House took over all private lighthouses in 1836, the practice began of sending items for repair to Trinity House at Tower Hill—a tendency made possible by the greater efficiency of the postal service at the time, and later the coming of the railways. Later on this work was sent to Blackwall to be handled by a small group of tradesmen under a man named Wallace. This work was done on board an old hulk named *Africa*, moored in the river and to which the Trinity tenders moored when returning to their base there.

There is a large flight of stone steps at the river frontage of the depot for landing people from rowing boats and other small craft. It is believed to have been the embarkation point, before Trinity House acquired it, of convicts being sent out to British Colonies. These people were imprisoned in barracks located inside the East India Dock area while awaiting transportation. The heavily guarded gate which they used was still there when I first joined the Service and was only a few hundred yards from these steps.

For the historically minded reader there is another, more famous, embarkation point about one mile up river from these steps which is marked by a commemorative plaque. This is where the *Mayflower* embarked some of her passengers before proceeding to Plymouth for her final departure for America.

When James Douglass, later Sir James, was made Engineer in Chief in 1862, after the sudden death of Mr Walker their Consultant Engineer, he advised the Board that they should build their own workshops at Blackwall. This was agreed and in 1869 the workshops were erected and the site was considerably extended in 1870. These were developed into a whole range of specialist shops: blacksmiths, chain makers, coppersmiths, carpenters, painters, fitters, turners, pattern makers, electricians, radio engineers and others. Ship's anchor cables had been made of hemp rope prior to 1820, but with the introduction of chain it made good sense for Trinity House to have its own facility for making and proving (testing) the enormous quantity of chain required for all the buoys and lightship stations. When the Blackwall depot was closed in 1988 I believe the proving house for testing new chain was still there, although used for some other purpose. It has since become a listed building.

There was also another specialist piece of equipment at Blackwall—a plant which made gas from oil. This supplied oil gas in huge cylinders which the tenders then carried to sea and the gas was pumped into the lighted buoys to fuel their lanterns. The gas was stored in the buoy body at a pressure of six atmospheres and fed to the gas mantle inside the lantern.

These lanterns were made at the workshops and were very efficient, made of cast bronze and weighing just over 100 lbs. The gas mechanism released a charge to the pilot light to conform with the character allotted to its particular station. This small charge was then immediately burnt in the gas mantle suspended in the heavy lid of the lantern and could be seen at a range of 3 to 4 miles I recall that it was fiendishly difficult to light the pilot in windy conditions. One had to strike a match, light the pilot and close the lid quickly before the wind either blew out the pilot or else broke the flimsy mantle. The lid was very heavy, to withstand the waves which battered it at times, so was quite capable of chopping off a finger tip if you had it in the wrong place and were a bit careless. These oil gas buoys were the start of the lighted buoys and the first one was laid at the East Oaze station in the Thames Estuary in 1860. They continued in use until almost the outbreak of World War II, being gradually replaced from September 1916 when the first lighted buoy to use dissolved acetylene gas was laid at the Bahama Bank station off the Isle of Man. The acetylene came from large cylinders carried in pockets built into the buoy body. They have in turn been superseded by lanterns powered by solar panels; these can operate for four years with minimal attention and have considerably decreased the work of servicing these lighted buoys.

The marine side of the Blackwall depot continued for years and existed quite happily alongside the workshops establishment. The marine side organised the lightship reliefs and cleaning and repainting of buoys brought in from sea while the workshops concentrated on the repair of any damaged buoys or any equipment sent in from lighthouses and lightships from around the coast. At one time there were four tenders attached to Blackwall but this had been reduced to one named *Alert* when I was based there soon after joining the Service. The other three were then at the Harwich depot.

In 1874 and possibly earlier, Trinity House had victualled their ships and lightships using the same weekly scale of food as supplied to Merchant ships. Some items of this scale, per man, were: 8¾ lbs of meat, 2 lbs of flour, 7 lbs of potatoes, 2 oz of tea, 3 gallons of beer, or an allowance in lieu of 19s 6d per quarter.

There was a fully equipped butcher's shop at Blackwall to deal with these provisions, still there in 1939 although no longer in use. It was complete with rows of hooks and several butcher's blocks where carcases were cut up. It only disappeared after World War II when the marine side was moved permanently to Harwich and the Workshops were expanded to fill the whole site. The supply of food to ships' crews was discontinued in 1891 in favour of a victualling allowance of 1s 9d per day to all ratings and 2s 3d to all officers.

This system too was altered in 1912 and the victualling allowance became part of a man's wages and was then subject to income tax. This meant that all the tenders had to adopt the system known as 'weekly feeding' which all the coastal trading ships used. It simply meant that each man was responsible for bringing his own food each week for the cook to deal with, a most haphazard arrangement but it worked.

The officers' steward would buy the food for their mess and then presented each man with a bill at the end of the week. This arrangment lasted until 1970 when the system changed again as will be recounted later.

Reverting to the Blackwall Workshops it may surprise some Trinity House personnel to know that in the early years of the Workshops' existence the men in charge were fully qualified marine engineers with an Extra Chief's Certificate. Even up to the end of World War II no fitter or turner was employed unless he had a sea-going Chief Engineer's Certificate, which is a slightly inferior grade.

There was also a medium size replica of a lighthouse at this depot which is now a listed building and is no longer owned by Trinity House. In the early years of its existence the lighthouse was used for experimental work in the development of new lighting equipment and subsequently became a training place for new recruits to the Lighthouse Service. It was also used for several years by Michael Faraday, famous physicist, for many of his experiments.

After the start of World War II the marine section at Blackwall was moved to the Harwich depot but the process was spread over six years.

Prior to 1940 Harwich was just a sub-depot in importance to Blackwall. The main depot at Blackwall was where the Chief Superintendent was based and lived in a fine house on the premises. The early months of World War II were very quiet with regard to enemy activity in the London area. Almost all action was at sea or over the East Coast. Trinity House decided it would be safer for all their personnel attached to the Harwich depot to be transferred to the one in London. This included the crews of tenders and lightships on the Harwich District plus many of those working on the depot and of course all the families.

Trinity Wharf, Blackwall *(Illustrated London News)*

The Buoy Store, Trinity Wharf *(Illustrated London News)*

Fitting shop and Boiler shop.

Radio and Electrical shops.

Workshops from mid-stream.

Workshops frontage, buoys galore for overhaul and repair.

(photographs by J. Ridgeon)

This was a lengthy operation since it involved a great deal of house hunting and furniture removal at the appropriate time. However before it was completed the blitz on London began in the autumn of 1940 and eventually Blackwall received much damage. It included at least two unexploded bombs which are believed to be still on the site. This concentrated the mind of the Trinity House Board quite rapidly and everyone was transferred back to Harwich, plus the sea-going men of the London District—the men of the tender and the lightship crews. After the war it was decided to make this transfer permanent and to remove all marine stores and equipment to Harwich.

This operation was very time consuming and involved very many trips by the tenders to transfer all buoy equipment and spares, together with nearly a century's accumulation of redundant equipment—which included four old Lee Enfield rifles issued in World War I for sinking mines. These were found in the rafters of a store, still carefully wrapped in oiled cloth. Close by was a ship's figurehead which once graced a yacht's bow. It was believed to belong to the Trinity House ship *Irene* which was sunk in the First World War and whose figurehead had been removed for safe keeping at the outbreak of hostilities.

Another astonishing discovery was made when a huge stockpile of mooring chain, several hundred tons of it, was moved. This chain was always neatly piled in a large square shape in order to make the pile stable and as compact as possible, and perhaps 12 or 15 feet high at times. Upon removal it was found to have sunk over 12 inches into the ground because of its weight. In consequence it 'delivered up' several hundred fathoms more chain than it was supposed to contain!

The workshop's establishment continued until the relatively recent programme of automating the lightships and many of the lighthouses. It closed in 1988. The end came suddenly and the dedicated band of men employed there are now part of history although it will be the end of this century before the last station is automated. There were then about 150 personnel in total, of which some 55 were known as out-station personnel. These were mechanics, electricians, radio engineers and assistants. They were employed in the workshops until required, often at very short notice, to drop everything and proceed to deal with technical problems on any station. It was the dedication of such men as well as those in uniform on the stations who contributed to the reputation of the Trinity House Service for reliability.

These men often had to take with them heavy items of equipment and a remarkable number of tools. These latter were in a stout box, easily recognised and well known to all London railway stations. They were said to have magical properties because their appearance on any platform seemed to ensure the instant disappearance of every porter!

This of course was the least of their worries. That reputation for reliability meant that they were expected to respond at once, on receipt of instructions, to attend any breakdown of equipment. Such instruction could come at any time, day or night from the Workshop's Superintendent if it was a real emergency. This could mean an engineer must travel at daybreak to the workshops, pick up tools and any replacement parts needed and make his way to the station concerned.

If he was lucky that station might be on shore somewhere, such as the Lizard lighthouse or Flamborough Head. In which case he might be allowed to take his own car. But if it was an off-shore station he would need to go by train and rendezvous with the District tender perhaps or seek out a local boatman if the station was close inshore. Before the advent of helicopters this could be very protracted and unpleasant if the weather was bad. There were many occasions when a man arrived on the station wet through after a dirty trip in a boat. Occasionally he might also arrive without some of his repair material, if the boatman declined to make a second run into the landing place after seeing how difficult it was to get the Blackwall man ashore.

Things were very different after the helicopter was introduced to the Service from 1976 onwards. The first station to be fitted with a helicopter landing platform above the lantern was the Wolf Rock Lighthouse off Land's End. It was an immediate success and as each station was up-dated in turn it became the normal procedure to effect the monthly relief of the Keepers by this means and also to send out visiting maintenance personnel. It also enabled the programme of automating both lighthouses and lightships to proceed and this will reach its conclusion before the end of the century. There will be more on this subject in the lighthouse chapter.

Wolf Rock Lighthouse: it is no surprise that before a helicopter landing platform was installed, maintenance personnel could not always be landed.
(R.A.F., St Mawgan)

Chapter 3

My First Year at Sea

My career with Trinity House began with the signing of my Indenture to become an Apprentice for four years. Prior to this I found temporary employment after leaving school and waiting to sign up as a film extra on the making of *Goodbye Mr Chips*! For this I was paid the princely sum of one guinea per day (£1.10p), considerably more than I was to earn as an apprentice which turned out to be 1s 7d (7½p) per week! But I must add in fairness to my employers that I also received a free kit of uniforms and other clothing, as well as free food.

Every apprentice in this service received the same generosity which was quite unique, I believe, amongst ship owners as I never heard of any other such arrangement.

Some weeks after the sealing of my Indenture I was instructed to join my first ship, the *Patricia* at the Trinity House depot at Blackwall in London's dockland. Her base was actually at Harwich but she was visiting London for some other reason that day. About a month later I was transferred from *Patricia* at Harwich to the *Alert* which was

Patricia, the Trinity House flagship built in 1937, painted grey during the war to make her less conspicuous to aircraft. She was sold in 1980.

attached to the Blackwall depot. She looked after the buoys and lightships in the Thames Estuary and the Dover Straits and my grounding in navigation and the specialised work of the Trinity House Service began in earnest. This meant helping to clean, paint and service the never-ending numbers of buoys in the Thames Estuary and Dover Straits, which was *Alert's* particular patch, plus watch-keeping on the Bridge when steaming between jobs and helping with ship's maintenance work as required. No task was too onerous or dirty for an apprentice to be assigned to tackle it!

The Indenture which I signed on 31 January 1939, and which I still have, of course, is quite an imposing document. Printed on parchment and signed by Sir Arthur Morrell, the Deputy Master of Trinity House, it contains a whole list of 'do's and don'ts' which are best condensed here. First I was instructed to bind myself Apprentice to the said Master, Wardens and Assistants to learn the art, trade or business of a MARINER or SEAMAN . . . to remain and serve afloat and on shore . . . until the full end and term of FOUR YEARS etc. I was to well and truly obey and faithfully serve my Masters, their secrets keep and their lawful commands . . . on all occasions perform and execute.

I was not allowed to frequent Taverns or Ale-Houses nor play at cards or dice or any unlawful game. I was not to be guilty of profane swearing or drunkenness. I could not buy or sell goods without proper permission. I could not 'embezzle or waste any of my Master's goods'. I could not marry (some hopes on a wage of one shilling and seven pence per week!) nor absent myself, day or night, from the service of my Masters. I was, to the best of my ability, to perform, execute, do and apply myself to all and every work or business of my employers either by day or night, either afloat or ashore etc, etc.

In return my employers promised to 'cause the said Apprentice to be well and sufficiently taught, instructed and informed in the art, trade or business of a Mariner or Seaman and to provide him with suitable and sufficient meat, drink, lodging, apparel and washing for four years'. There was quite a bit more legal jargon too. I have since seen a similar Indenture that was signed by a Merchant Service ship-owner and his apprentices and was intrigued by one slight difference. Instead of not being allowed to frequent simple Taverns or Ale-houses as I was, they were debarred from Taverns, Ale-Houses and Houses of Ill Repute. I have never discovered why the latter were omitted from my Indenture—perhaps the Elder Brethren had never heard of their existence! Or did they think it would be a waste of time in the case of their own apprentices?

Trinity House tender *Alert* in earlier times—a painting circa 1900.
(from *Life at Sea*)

There was a second apprentice on the *Alert* who had already served his first year so I was able to learn quite a lot from him. Apart from the work already described we were also required to study navigation and seamanship manuals and to learn chartwork. This was in preparation for obtaining a Second Mate's Certificate at the end of the apprenticeship which was a major hurdle in our progress to becoming a deck officer.

One other important task was to study all the seamarks on the London District from Gravesend to North Foreland and right down to Dungeness which meant all the buoys, beacons, lighthouses and lightships. We had to learn by heart all characteristics of their colours, shapes, lights, fog signals, depth of water, fairway courses and distances in all the different channels and a host of other information. This was in preparation for a Pilotage Examination, after three years' study, to be carried out by one of the Elder Brethren. We had to pass this examination before we were allowed to sit for the Second Mate's Certificate.

There were two further examinations in Pilotage as we progressed in the Service, a slightly harder one for the rank of First Officer and a final one, considerably harder, for the rank of Master which covered questions on another District plus a general knowledge of seamarks and other details on all the Trinity House Districts. All this was in addition to the Board of Trade examinations for the ranks of Second Mate, Mate and Master. It included, naturally, learning 'the art, trade or business of a mariner or seaman', such as chipping and painting, splicing rope, heaving the lead and a hundred other things.

One special duty that the apprentices had was attending to the flags. This meant raising the ensign promptly at 8.00 am in summer and 9.00 am in winter. Plus any special flag such as the Elder Brother's Jack or the Superintendent's Cornet if we had one of these dignitaries on board. During any time the ship was under way one of us had to watch out for any H.M. ship passing and dip our ensign to her. We also had to watch out for any lightship which we passed who should dip her ensign to us and we had to respond.

This early period of my career was full of interest and I enjoyed it immensely. It was quite unlike life on a Merchant ship which went away for months or even a year or two at a time, nor indeed did it bear much resemblance to life on a small coaster although the ships were similar in size. For one thing we were a uniformed Service and were expected to wear it at all times, afloat or ashore in the case of apprentices since it was provided by our employer. The crews also had uniform provided but mostly wore dungarees except on special occasions when full rig was called for.

Light vessel dips her ensign to Trinity House tender *Stella* which has just completed delivering of stores to the light vessel and is now leaving.

(N.W. Fitkin)

The officers and apprentices all ate together and on most of the Trinity House ships, including the *Alert*, we dressed for dinner in the evenings. This soon ceased after the outbreak of war when our ships were attacked quite often and it was pointless to take the extra uniforms when you might lose everything on the next trip to sea.

I believe every one of the nine ships in the Trinity House fleet was attacked during the second world war, some of them several times and four of them were sunk by mines. Two of them with no loss of life fortunately, but the others suffered a considerable loss. More details of wartime activity can be found in a later chapter, but now might be an appropriate time to mention one piece of great good fortune that I enjoyed early in the war.

This was the time of the so-called 'Phoney War' which of course was a stupid name as far as people at sea were concerned. I was still on the *Alert* and working in the Thames Estuary area and she was sent to work near Harwich in November 1939. By then we knew all about magnetic mines and a great many ships had already been sunk by them. About mid-day on November 21st we saw a Japanese passenger liner, named *Terukuni Maru*, mined just ahead of us near the Sunk lightship, off Essex. She was badly damaged and began listing over and sinking almost at once. We were soon close to her and sent our motor boats away to bring back her lifeboats full of survivors. I had previously been given an old Kodak Brownie camera and managed to capture the whole scene. As soon as the survivors, about 120 people, were safely on board *Alert*, plus the boats which we hoisted on board to prevent them being a hazard to other ships, we steamed for Harwich to land them. Japan was still a neutral country of course and had her national flag painted boldly on her side to deter air attacks. Several other ships picked up survivors and nobody was lost.

When we reached port the news had already gone round that we were bringing them in and I met a reporter from the *Daily Mirror* on the quayside who sent my roll of film immediately to London where it was in time for the following day's papers. I was astonished to see the picture that I took right across the centre page with a paragraph about my initiative! The picture earned me £100 plus a further £76 as my share of what it earned when sold around the world. Today such sums would be chicken feed for a scoop picture, but it was an immense sum for an impecunious apprentice.

The scoop picture taken from the *Alert* of the sinking of the *Terukuni Maru* off Waiton-on-the-Naze. Note the Japanese flag painted on her hull. All neutral ships did this to prevent possible attack from the air, but it was useless to prevent being mined, whatever nationality it was. As a result she was the last Japanese ship to trade to Britain for many years.

Fortunately for me no mention of my ship or its owners was made in the paper or I might have earned my first reprimand for giving information to the press without official sanction.

There was one surprising twist to this story which only came to my notice some 48 years later, after my retirement. The Japanese captain was a direct descendant of the famous Cornish Mining Engineer Richard Trevithick and was his great grandson. This line began when one of Trevithick's sons, who was a railway engineer, went out to Japan in the mid 1800s to build their railway system. He settled out there, married a local girl and his son and grandson bore his name. But his great grandson had to change his name to a Japanese one, Okuno, when he became a Captain in the Japanese Merchant Navy. Years later I became a member of the Trevithick Society in Cornwall and had the pleasure of meeting Frank Okuno, son of the liner's captain. What a small world.

I have another abiding wartime memory from this same period when I was on the *Alert* at Blackwall in November 1939. There was a dry dock next door to the Trinity depot and their river frontage was of course continuous with that of the Trinity one. Some sudden fear of enemy sabotage caused the authorities to place an armed guard on the entrance to that dock and all others on the Thames. No warning was passed to the personnel on the Trinity depot as far as I was aware. I went ashore to the cinema and returned about 9.00 pm in pitch darkness and low water, which entailed walking across the foreshore. After shouting to the ship's night watchman to send the small boat for me I began picking my way across the stones towards him. Suddenly I froze in my tracks at the sound of a rifle bolt being slammed home and a shout of 'halt or I fire' from the dockside just above me! Fortunately my fruity reply convinced him I was not the enemy and I lived to tell the tale.

When I joined in 1939 there were Trinity House depots at Holyhead, Swansea, Penzance, Cowes, London, Harwich and Great Yarmouth. Later in my career I served on all districts administered by them. There had been other depots in the past, at Burton (near Neyland in Milford Haven) which still exists but is not owned by Trinity House, and at Cardiff, Littlehampton, Ramsgate and Wells in the Wash.

There was also a very small base, not a depot, at Tresco in the Isles of Scilly for attending to the relief of the Seven Stones lightship. This was established in 1841 at the same time that the lightship was first laid on station. Most of her crew, two Masters and eleven seamen at that time, were accommodated on the island and the small tender used for the relief was moored in the tiny harbour there.

The lightship station is about nine miles from the islands and thirty miles from Penzance so Tresco was a very convenient location. At least it was until 1866 when a series of letters began, between the Board of Trinity House and the landowner of Tresco, Mr Augustus Smith, about the difficulty of housing their people properly. This correspondence became increasingly acid in content although couched in rather flowery language as used by Gentlemen in the 1800s and was only terminated in 1868 when Trinity House withdrew all the lightship crew and housed them at Penzance.

Mr Smith was so incensed by this outcome that he published all the letters in a pamphlet at his own expense. A copy of it, dated 1868 and printed in London, is still in the Truro Museum. He also demanded a full and impartial inquiry by the Board of Trade, but there is no mention of him receiving it.

Before I was married I lived on the tender attached to the depot where I was serving and after marriage had a house at all of them except Swansea. These transfers from one District to another happened to many of the Officers in the Service and almost always came with little or no warning in advance for anyone. The worst one, for me, occurred in August 1940 while I was on the *Alert* at Blackwall. I was summoned to go ashore one Saturday morning to see the Superintendent. He informed me that I had been transferred to the ship at Swansea and I was to return on board, pack all my bags and catch the 1.00 pm train from Paddington. He must have seen my face fall because he added as an afterthought, 'I'll arrange a taxi to be here for 12 o'clock for you, so get a move on.' It may of course have been a blessing in disguise since it meant that I escaped the Blitz on London.

Something similar happened to me in 1966 at Harwich after I had been in Command for several years. I was told one Friday that I was transferred to the ship at Penzance and was required to travel on the

The Trinity House depot at Burton near Neyland, no longer owned by Trinity House. (photo: *The Western Telegraph*)

following Monday. Things had improved slightly since 1940 as the Superintendent did apologise for the short notice! This moving of officers from District to District ensured, of course, that one received a good mix of experience since the daily routine was different as between the East Coast and West Coast Districts. On the East it was basically shallow water and many sand banks. There were therefore a great many buoys and a great number of lightships. On the West Coast the water is deep, virtually no sand banks with buoys to mark them but plenty of rocks and lighthouses. In the west there are much greater distances between stations too, whereas the East Coast tenders could work all day on buoy maintenance and only move about twelve miles between each night's anchorage.

There was also a 'rolling programme' of dry-docking for lightships when each one in turn had to be replaced by a spare ship and towed to the repair yard for dry-docking and repair. All British lightships were 'dumb', that is, with no means of propulsion. On each District the tenders were always 'on call' to attend the unexpected casualty. It might be a buoy damaged by collision, an engine breakdown on lightship or lighthouse or a human one caused by illness or injury. This latter could involve a visit to the station by the ship or a protracted discussion over the radio to try and diagnose the complaint using the *Ship Captain's Medical Guide* for reference. This is a famous Board of Trade publication which offers medical advice on all kinds of ailments.

Prior to the introduction of radio at Trinity House stations the men in charge of them had to rely on this book, plus common sense and the contents of the Board of Trade medical cabinet. Reliance too, I believe, on the well known 'Plimsoll Line' method of diagnosis. You asked where the pain was and, depending on whether it was above or below the navel, he received an emetic or a purgative. I don't think this treatment ever proved fatal!

There were other emergencies of a much more distressful nature too, fortunately rare. Cases of suicide on lightships by jumping overboard or hanging in the chain locker, or men jumping or falling from lighthouses. Occasionally there were cases of men simply missing from an isolated station, leaving the dreadful uncertainty of 'did he fall or was he pushed?' With only three men on a lighthouse and one of them asleep who knows what violent argument might arise between the other two, resulting in a tragedy to one of them.

These incidents were of course reported to Trinity House and were also recorded in the Station Order Book, as such logs were called. The Bishop Rock lighthouse has two such laconic entries: 19th December 1898, 'Principal Keeper J Ball was missed this afternoon', and again for 13th August 1903, 'Assistant Keeper S R Hicks accidentally drowned'.

Not all of these sad deaths were connected to the lightships or lighthouses. One senior officer on a tender shot himself in the 1920s using the Lee Enfield rifle supplied for sinking floating mines. There was even a suicide from the top of Trinity House itself in the early 1900s when a Secretary threw himself over the parapet of the flat roof.

One man named Davies was drowned at the Eddystone in August 1929 having fallen off the landing while receiving a present of fish from a small boat. Fortunately such incidents were uncommon but in a period of almost 300 years the toll was quite considerable.

As mentioned previously, work on the East Coast tenders was a long round of buoy work and lightship reliefs. Both activities involved a great deal of boat work which was also experienced on the West Coast at the lighthouses. It was this continual small boat employment which produced the envied reputation held by Trinity seamen for their boat handling skill. It also produced some fear and trepidation in new personnel who joined the Service from passenger liners and other foreign going ships and had no experience of lowering and recovering boats in rough weather. There was a considerable expertise required from all concerned in the operation, from the Captain downwards. He needed to provide a good 'lee' when the boat was lowered or lifted and the men manning the rope falls or wire hoist had to act swiftly on the word of command given by the officer controlling the operation. The boat's crew were well used to the crash and thump as they hit the water and again when being lifted out if the ship was rolling heavily. But the passengers were often quite terrified on a bad day.

The poor lighthouse keepers never really got used to it. That is not surprising when you realise that their station never moved and was as steady as the rock on which it was built, apart from the hideous shudder they felt in bad weather when a really huge wave struck the tower. I am reminded of an amusing story told by the Penzance Superintendent when a newspaper reporter rang up for some details of the Eddystone lighthouse and its keepers. One question he asked was 'I suppose they are all expert navigators?' At which the Superintendent nearly exploded with the retort, 'Of course they aren't, they're not going anywhere!'

Relief in progress at Wolf Rock lighthouse, using the rope hoist.
This Derrick had to be completely dismantled after each period of use and only the heavy steel post would be left on the platform.

The lighthouse keeper being lifted out of the ship's boat at Round Island lighthouse.

Chapter 4

The Lightship Service

Returning to the early months of 1939 the peacetime work for *Alert* at Blackwall was a routine of three weeks on buoy work and one on the lightship relief, with occasional weekend work if there was a casualty to one of those stations.

The 'relief' was a well established routine commencing about mid-day on a Monday and occurred at every one of the Trinity House depots around the coast of England and Wales. Similar routines occurred in the Irish and Scottish lighthouse services of course but they are not under Trinity House jurisdiction.

The work began with loading bags of coal, drums of oil, paint, stores and sometimes items of repaired equipment. About mid-day the lightsmen appeared with their personal gear and their food for four weeks. There were then eleven lightships on the London District which extended as far as Folkestone, plus the Chapman lighthouse in Sea Reach. Each had a crew of nine men who served eight weeks on board and four ashore with three men changing over every four weeks, plus two Masters who did month and month about. So there was a considerable crowd of men and the ship seemed alive with extra voices and new faces.

Only two years earlier in 1937 their routine had included working at the depot during their time ashore, cleaning and re-painting buoys that had been brought in from sea for overhaul or repair. They were also 'on call' to man any spare lightship required to replace one on station that was due for dry-docking or overhaul. This could mean several days, even a week or more, between leaving port with the spare lightship, exchanging her on station and then taking the Station ship to the dockyard. All this was taken from a man's so-called shore leave period—not much of a holiday after a monotonous eight weeks at anchor.

Some of the men were employed as 'houseman' at the two dwellings on some depots occupied by the Superintendent and the Storekeeper

The Trinity House ship *Satellite* approaching the *Seven Stones* lightship off Land's End. She is 'passing up' a heavy duty rope hawser to make fast to the stern of the lightship.
(Photographed in the inter-war years)

with their families. This routine was followed at all the depots in the Service and the lightsmen had struggled for many years to get the Board to relax this regime.

There is a letter still in existence dated 2nd July 1872 from the Superintendent at Blackwall reporting to Trinity House that 18 lightsmen on the London District had 'refused to go to sea the day previously stating that they had done a hard day's work and would not go until the morning'. The Board's reply is not on record but it took 65 years before they relented and changed the system. That same routine in the 1930s at the Great Yarmouth depot also included manning the depot steam launch when she was sometimes required to attend on some of the nearby lightships or to do some survey work in Yarmouth Roads. For this they received the princely sum of 2s 6d for six hours spent at sea, and they would literally fight for the chance to be selected. This is more a reflection on their low rate of pay rather than an indication of their zeal for extra work.

The appropriate 'Depot Ditty' ran :

A lightsman's life is full of joys,
Like late reliefs and chipping buoys;
Two months at sea on the end of a chain,
Then a month ashore on the 10-ton crane.

Broadly speaking it isn't bliss,
When you come to think of this!
And 'nothing good' I've heard him say,
'Can come of this 'ere cut in pay.'

When on shore he mans the store,
Eight till five (and sometimes more!)
Today he's painter, tomorrow cook;
After that pulls chain with hook.

When, of course, he's out at sea,
He's quite content, (or ought to be!)
If by chance, he gets the 'blues',
He 'listens' in for Local News.

The cut in pay was almost certainly a reference to the notorious 'Geddy's axe'. This was a proposal by a Government Minister of that name in the early 1920s that the Civil Service should all accept a wage cut which would certainly have affected pay in the Trinity House Service.

This delightful poem appeared only a few weeks before World War II and made a big impression on me as a young apprentice. This was partly, I suppose, because I had to spend so many hours memorising the particular characteristics of lightships.

Lightships
(Air : Bonny Dundee, Cockles and Mussels, or what you will)

The *Tongue* and the *Girdler*, the *Mouse* and the *Nore*,
They lead the bold seaman to London's fair shore,
And it's time that the praises of seamen were sung,
To the *Nore* and the *Girdler*, the *Mouse* and the *Tongue*.

A light, A light O'!
A light, A light O',
The Tongue and the Girdler,
A light, A light O'.

The life of the ocean holds many a curse
But in unpleasant weather few things can be worse,
Than tossing at anchor in sight of the shore
As they do in the *Girdler*, the *Mouse* and the *Nore*.

The sailors go by into tempest and dread
Their home is astern and the ocean's ahead,
But each one is thankful he is not among
The crew of the *Girdler*, the *Mouse* or the *Tongue*.

We sailed out of Rotterdam and into the fog,
No sailor was happy, not even the dog.
But high were our hearts when about us there swung,
The embracing, exciting, great arms of the *Tongue*.

We took Prince's Channel and said we're at home
Nor never no more over sea will we roam.
But settle down at Shoebury and buy a fine house,
With a view of the *Nore* and the jolly red *Mouse*.

The Chapman, the Muckings, are welcoming lights,
The Blyths and the Ovens congenial sights,
But where is the sailor would set them before
The first glimpse of the *Girdler*, the *Mouse* and the *Nore*?

So let every mariner that ever was fain
To come through the storm to old England again,
Toss off a full bumper to Trinity House
For the *Tongue*, and the *Girdler*, the *Nore* and the *Mouse*!

O blest be their sirens, their bells and their buoys,
It's true that they make a lugubrious noise.
But they sound like sweet music on England's fair shore—
And especially the *Girdler*, the *Tongue* and the *Nore*.

A light, A light O' , etc, etc.

(With acknowledgements to A P Herbert. This was first published in *Punch* in 1939)

The four lightships in the first verse have, sadly, all been replaced by buoys now and the Chapman, which was a pile lighthouse near Canvey Island was removed in 1957. The Muckings, Ovens and Blyths are all buoys in the lower reaches of the Thames and still exist.

My first contact with the *Mouse* lightship was in 1936, some time before I even knew about Trinity House. My brother and I had a week's holiday with friends in a small cabin cruiser in the Thames Estuary, in the course of which we sailed from Sheerness to Harwich and passed close to the *Mouse* in quite sunny weather. We waved and shouted to the men on deck and collected letters from them for posting, thrown to us in passing, tied in a rolled up newspaper. However, we did not stop as the fog signal was sounding, making conversation difficult. We supposed they were testing the signal but several years later when I was an apprentice I learned that the men on board all received an extra 2d for every hour the signal sounded and had been recorded on a special graph. So naturally it was kept sounding until every vestige of fog or mist, real or imaginary, was dispelled! Years later I met one of the Service mechanics whose father had been a lightship Master. He told me that he and his brother 'were brought up on fog-money'. The signal had to be sounded of course to use up the oil that had to be expended to keep the books straight.

The Lightship Master (Bless his soul),
Worries about his oil and coal.
Daily as he writes his log,
He totals up the hours of fog.
And if it's thick with mist or rain,
He starts the foghorn up again.
To him is given the legal power,
Of saving up two pence per hour!

Some years later Trinity House decided to stop this Fog Allowance money and to pay a 'consolidated' amount of money in the lightsmen's wages instead. So less oil was expended and it appeared that Trinity House found they saved a staggering amount of money on their yearly oil bill! In fairness to the crews I should mention that before World War II the wages for a seaman were £11 0s 5d per month, which equates to 36 pence per day in today's money. This had to suffice for a man to keep his wife and family and bear the cost of a man's food for his month afloat. So two pence an hour for the inconvenience of having to put up with the raucous noise seems rather paltry. This extra payment was also known as 'fog dust'.

The lightship Master served one month aboard and one ashore so there was a big incentive for a man to study and become proficient enough to be made Master in due course. One of the Master's duties when the Lightship Service began was to conduct an informal service on Sundays. For this purpose each lightship was issued with a Bible, several prayer books and also a book of sermons. Each of these books was beautifully bound in leather and embossed with the Trinity House Crest and the name of the station. The same arrangement also applied to the tenders if they were at sea on a Sunday but I believe this practice died out as a result of World War I. Many of these books have survived at Trinity House but they show very little sign of having been used, only signs of old age!

During the 19th century and early part of the 20th most lightship hulls were all wood and were quite a modest size. Thus the ones stationed at the most exposed positions such as the *Seven Stones* off Lands End, the *St Govan* at the entrance to the Bristol Channel or the *Humber* at the approaches to that river were subject to damage in very severe weather. As a result such stations carried a stock of timber plus a very well stocked tool chest ready for any emergency.

The Seven Stones lightship, situated almost halfway between the Isles of Scilly and Lands End records just such an occasion in her log book on 29th December 1900 when she suffered very severe storm damage. A large section of her bulwarks was carried away and one of her boats was torn from its chocks and smashed against one of her ventilators. In doing so it jammed one of the crew and tore off a piece of his thigh. Another man received a cut on his face from his eyebrow to his chin.

Two shipwrights were put on board on 1st February and took nearly three weeks to repair the damage. Another sad entry, for 12th June 1908, records that seaman Richards fell off the main deckhouse and died from a broken neck.

Her log book also records three occasions when survivors of wrecks on the reef were rescued. On 21st December 1887 the Superintendent arrived to inspect the station and found eight men from the *S S Brighouse* on board. On 6th February 1891 he again found survivors on board, two officers and six seamen from *S S Cheswick* sunk on 5th February. On another occasion, not fully recorded, the lightship rescued no fewer than 25 men from the boats of *S S Camiola*.

All these incidents were before the use of radio of course, so contact with the shore was dependant on a homeward bound vessel being close enough to the lightship to be given a message. But this would be very rare since any sailing ship would be highly unlikely to be that close to a lightship known to be marking a highly dangerous reef. In fact *Seven Stones* was one of those stations which carried a large topmark at its masthead for the very reason that sailing ships could identify her by telescope at a range of several miles and should never need to get close.

This lightship was witness to one of the worst maritime disasters ever to happen around our shores. This was the stranding of the *Torrey Canyon* tanker on the Seven Stones reef in broad daylight on 18th March 1967. Her cargo of crude oil caused the worst pollution incident ever experienced up to that time.

Coal being loaded onto *Seven Stones* lightship

(Photo: N. W. Fitkin)

The lightship had attempted to warn her off the reef by firing her signal cannon, signalling by lamp and hoisting flag signals, but to no avail. The tanker was eventually bombed by the RAF to release the remainder of her oil so that it could be chemically treated. Fortunately there was no loss of life.

Since the lightship service began in 1732 there have been countless times when they have rendered help to passing ships, yachts or fishing boats who were perhaps lost in fog, damaged or just short of fuel.

The first lightship in 1732 was laid at the Nore in the entrance to the Thames by a man called Avery, against the advice of Trinity House who opposed the whole idea of lightships. But it proved to be a success and quickly became popular with mariners and ship owners. She was just a small collier with one mast and one cross yard, with a ship's lantern at each end. Within two years Trinity House had reversed its opinion and granted a lease of 61 years to Avery. (See *Keepers of the Sea* for the full story).

An early painting of *Nore* light vessel, the first lightship, laid at the mouth of the Thames in 1732.

After the lease expired Trinity House took over responsibility for the station and laid their own lightship there in 1794. There was then a slow but steady growth of lightship stations. Some were private ventures, the first being at the Dudgeon, Owers and North Goodwin stations. These were sometimes purpose built but were often sailing ships or fishing vessels adapted for the purpose.

It was not until the 1800s that Trinity House began seriously to expand the lightship service and built them to their own design. They also numbered them from No 1 in 1823 to No 95 in 1938. After the last war a new building programme started with No 1 again in 1946 and this ceased in 1967 with No 22. Since that time Trinity House has automated all those stations which are still marked by lightships and have sold off the major portion of lightships which they still owned.

In 1839 they built four new lightships which were numbered 12 to 15, number 14 being allocated to the Nore station just down river from Southend. In 1939 she was still moored at the same position and celebrated 100 years of continuous service there, apart from her regular dry-docking every seven years. (This period between dockings was reduced to three years for steel ships with more sophisticated equipment on board.) Some wag was reported as saying she was almost aground on her own empty milk tins!

Sadly she ended her days as a war casualty when she was sunk on 13th October 1944 off Beachy Head when on tow for some unrecorded purpose. She was the first lightship I ever stepped aboard when my career began and I can remember the interest she aroused in the local Press over her Centenary. She was not by any means the longest serving wooden lightship, however. Number 4 was built in 1831 and survived until 1948. For the last 20 years of her life she was moored at the Trinity depot in Great Yarmouth, being used as a storage for coal as well as a hulk for the tenders to moor alongside. She ended her days in a breakers' yard near the river mouth.

To return to the old *Nore* lightship the reader must forget any picture they may have seen of a modern lightship with power driven compressors and electricity generators, two berthed cabins and a powered windlass. The old number 14 had none of these for the whole of her existence. Only the Master had a separate cabin: everyone else slept in a hammock in the open forecastle. The only toilet was an unheated hut on the deck with no running water, just a bucket on a line. All lighting was by oil lamps, including the navigation light on the mast. The fog horn was entirely operated by an air compressor which was driven by the feet of the crew. The lantern was lowered every morning, by hand of course, in order to trim the wicks and clean the glass of all the oil lamps, and then raised again at nightfall. The windlass too was hand powered. It used to take about twelve strokes, by four men, on the massive handles to bring in just a couple of links of her heavy cable. You could barely see it moving as the windlass turned. Long before I first saw one of these windlasses and helped to man it when my ship was overhauling a cable, it had been dubbed as 'handraulic gear', also known as 'Armstrong's Patent'.

There was not a great deal of publicity given to the Service pre-war, as I have already indicated, which led to a rather silly misunderstanding at the outbreak of war in 1939 about ration books for the crew of the *Nore* lightship. All seafarers had a special book which allowed them extra rations, except for the crews of harbour or river craft. When three of the *Nore's* crew applied for their books at the Shipping Office they were told that they were not entitled to the Seaman's book because they were not outside the Thames, and in any case were home every night! This did not go down well at all with men who were just going to sea for eight weeks, and a row began to develop. Eventually the Clerk produced the official book which showed that the demarcation line between sea and river at the entrance to the Thames ran through the position of the Nore itself. It then had to be pointed out to the Clerk that the lightship always swung round with the tide, so how did a man manage if he spent every day half in and half out of each area? Fortunately an appeal to higher authority resolved the dilemma and the men received the book to which they were entitled.

Life on board that early class of lightship was rather monastic to say the least. No radio, no television, no newspapers, no letters, no fresh food except fish until the relief occurred, when the tender visited once a month to change over half the crew. There was then a change of library boxes, provided that the apprentice remembered to get it ready. These boxes were supplied by the British Sailors' Society and carried two

Recreation time on *Gull* light vessel, circa 1900.

(from *Life at Sea*)

dozen books which were usually welcomed by the crew. Not always though, because the system relied on the apprentice keeping a careful check to see that the boxes were properly rotated through the twelve stations on the district, so that each ship had a fresh box each relief. That was not all that easy, because the vagaries of the weather might mean that the Captain decided to go to the furthest lightship away from the depot and work in towards the nearest. Or maybe the tender might have to transfer a man from one station to another and would have to vary the order in which the reliefs were done. I can well remember getting the rough edge of somebody's tongue when he found the box he had just received was the very one he had read through on his previous turn of duty. This complaint was via a radio call just after we had finished the 'relief', but there was no chance whatever of our Captain returning just to exchange one library box.

I remember one leg-pull that was perpetrated on a lightship Master who was very superstitious. He was known to have a firm belief in Davey Jones' Locker waiting for him if he fell overboard. His cabin extended right across the width of the lightship with a porthole at each side. One quiet, misty evening some joker made a pair of imitation skeleton hands from some padded gloves with finger bones outlined in white. He then fastened them to a pair of boat-hooks so that the 'hands' were just outside the portholes, one each side, as if they were clutching the cabin in an attempt to drag it down into the sea. History has not recorded any comments from the poor chap below deck!

Before the coming of radio and later on the television, the crew's spare time occupations were very simple. Reading, card playing and work on hobbies. Mat making was a favourite one, together with model making and knitting. Items were usually made with a view to selling the results ashore to augment the men's pay.

After World War II the conditions began to improve as more modern lightships were designed and built. The building was stimulated, of course, by the loss of no less than 20 lightships during the war, fortunately many of which were unmanned for various reasons. The improvements made in these new lightships had their drawbacks, however. A lightship Master who had spent many years in an old ship without modern machinery could be very bewildered if he was

Mat-making on *Gull* light vessel at the beginning of this century.
(from *Life at Sea*)

transferred to a brand new ship with only a modest period of instruction beforehand. Sadly, the people in 'Head Office' had very little idea of the difficulties faced by a man who was nearing retirement having to learn new routines and different techniques. I well remember one bizarre accident which happened when the Yarmouth based tender was establishing a brand new lightship at the Smiths Knoll station in the North Sea in 1948.

The routine for this operation was fairly simple. The tender was gently towing the lightship up to her assigned position with her great anchor hanging below her keel ready to be dropped. On the word from our ship's bridge the lightship Master opened the windlass brake and away went the chain with a great roar. At the same time we slackened off the tow rope and they cast it off. Unfortunately, some piece of debris left in her chain locker—an old piece of rag perhaps—came flying up with the chain that startled the man on the windlass brake. He momentarily let go of the brake control, which allowed the outgoing chain to speed up. He then grabbed hold of the brake, and in his confusion opened it fully instead of closing it and jammed it open. The chain continued to fly out of the hawse pipe at vast speed, all 210 fathoms of it, until it burst open the shackle holding the end secure in the chain locker and it went flying down the hawsepipe. Within little more than 90 seconds the whole lot was piled on the sea bottom, the lightship was slowly drifting away from us and there was now dead silence.

The lightship of course had a spare anchor and cable which she dropped and then we spent four days searching for and recovering the lost gear, before finally finishing the job. Our Captain's comments are not repeatable.

The method of recovering the chain was by a laborious business of dragging a huge grapnel, which had four prongs and weighed almost a ton, attached to a chain, backwards and forwards across the position until we finally hooked into it. Since it had all gone down so quickly it lay in one great heap and was very difficult to find as a consequence.

This method of recovering lost chain was regularly used when lightships or buoys parted their cable for one reason or another. It was even used during World War II with much trepidation at the thought that we could conceivably hook into the mooring of a sunken mine. This did occur on one occasion but fortunately without triggering the mine. The incident was reported to Trinity House and resulted in two letters from 'on high'. The first was one of commendation on the action of the personnel concerned in freeing the ship from the dangerous object and is reproduced at the back of the book. The second was a circular letter to all ships to tell them of this incident and instructing the Captains to 'grapple with caution in future'.

No one quite knew how this instruction could be followed out and one Captain produced a design for a new grapnel with all four prongs turned inwards to ensure it could not possibly hook anything at all! He called it 'A Design for a Cautionary Grapnel' and sent it to Trinity House for approval. It only produced a dignified silence as far as I am aware.

There have been other amusing directives from Trinity House and while researching for this book I found one that was issued in World War I concerning aircraft. It was a directive sent to the four lightships marking the Goodwin Sands off Deal in 1915, instructing them to note any enemy aircraft passing within sight. This was to be noted in the logbook, with estimates of their height, speed, type and numbers, and this information was to be brought ashore 'at the next relief'. So it could therefore be anything up to four weeks old, since none were fitted with radio at that time.

Another directive also concerned aircraft and was sent to all shore-based light-houses in 1921. This instructed the keepers that if they were asked by any aircraft to sound the station fog signal when weather conditions did not call for it to be sounded the station was to start the signal as soon as possible and to pass the full details to Trinity House. It taxes the imagination to think any airman would navigate by the sound of one isolated fog signal blast.

From the commencement of the lightship service they nearly all had wooden hulls—until 1886, by which time 59 had been built. These were all fairly small ships ranging from 78 feet to 105 feet in length and 19 feet to 24 feet in breadth. There was however one exception to this, number 51 was much longer than any other at 123 feet. She was built as a three-masted sailing ship and went out to Ceylon to assist at the building of the Great and Little Basses lighthouses, probably doing duty as a barrack ship for the work force.

On her return to England her three masts were removed for her conversion to a lightship and the three holes left in her deck were made secure by the fitting of large circular deck lights which puzzled many crew members who were not aware of her history. She served at various stations around our coast until she was sunk at the Helwick station off the South Wales coast on 10th August 1943. She had been converted to an unmanned light float for the war period and the cause of her sinking is not recorded.

Another lightship which had her own peculiar distinction was the *Cockle* which used to mark the north entrance to Yarmouth Roads known as the Cockle Gatway. This is a rather narrow channel between two sandbanks which induce a very strong tidal flow.

As a result of that flow she always rode to a long scope of chain and was continually sheering from side to side on a strong Spring tide. If any unwary coaster should pass across her bows this would momentarily break the force of the tidal stream and the lightship's heavy cable would drop to the sea bed for a few seconds. This caused the lightship to forge violently ahead for a moment or two and give all the appearance of trying to ram the offending coaster, much to the consternation of her helmsman.

The crew of the *Cockle* devised a unique method of sending letters home which very seldom failed. They would write their letters in pencil, secure them between two pieces of wood and throw them overboard on a north-going tide. They eventually went ashore on the Norfolk coast anywhere between Winterton and Cromer and were invariably found by the beachcombers and posted, or sometimes delivered by hand, to the man's home. This may sound like a 'fisherman's tale' but I was assured of its truth by one of the lightship crew who used this method quite regularly.

Sadly this lightship was a witness of one of the worst peace-time accidents that any Trinity House ship suffered. One of the tasks that the Service had prior to 1950 was the dispersal of dangerous wrecks, having first located them, and surveyed them if possible. In February 1909 during a snowstorm a sailing barge was in collision with a ship called *Dundee* near the Cockle lightship and sank immediately with the loss of her crew, four men. The identity of the barge was not known but the Trinity ship *Argus* was detailed to locate the wreck, survey it and clear it if possible. It had gone down fairly close to the lightship so was likely to be a danger to shipping. The weather was too rough to carry out a survey but the work of clearing it commenced three days later.

One of the ship's boats carrying seven men began to lower explosives, Tonite charges, on to the wreck with the electric cable, which would be

Models of early lightships, all of which were lost in the fire at Trinity House in 1940.

used to detonate them to remove the mast and spars. When the charges were firmly 'snagged' into the wreck the boat was allowed to drift away several hundred yards and the charge was fired. This was done twice which resulted each time in blowing away small amounts of timber. The third attempt however, produced a tremendous explosion which sank the boat and killed six of the seven men. It also sent up a portion of the barge with her name on it and the subsequent enquiry revealed that she carried a mixed cargo, one portion of it being 15 tons of gelignite.

The explosion was so great that it was heard several miles inland and the shock was thought to be an earthquake in some of the villages. The lightship received considerable damage as a result of the explosion but was able to put her boat down in an attempt to recover some of the bodies being swept away by the tide. The local newspaper carried considerable coverage of this disaster and also carried a sly dig at Trinity House Regulations concerning contact with the Press! Under a by-line, 'AS SEEN BY AN EYE-WITNESS', the paper wrote: 'The strict regulations forbidding members of the Trinity Service to hold communication with those desperately dangerous persons, newspaper reporters, has rendered the gathering of facts a matter of some difficulty, but in one way and another a member of our staff has gleaned and pieced together the details of the tragic affair . . .' A fund was set up by the Mayor of Yarmouth for the benefit of the dependents of those lost and Trinity House contributed £500, quite a considerable sum in those days. It was in addition to the pension that the widows received.

This method of removing small wrecks was used right up to the outbreak of World War II when it was suspended during the hostilities. Afterwards the task of dispersing the hundreds of wrecks around our coasts was taken over by the Admiralty as Agents for Trinity House until 1958. Since then Trinity House has used commercial salvage companies as their Agents for any wreck dispersal required.

The responsibility for removing dangerous wrecks around England and Wales was laid on Trinity House by the Merchant Shipping Act of 1894 and that duty still applies. In the period from 1894 to the outbreak of World War I the average number of wrecks dispersed was about 80 per year. The explosive used by Trinity House until 1940 was Tonite and it was fired by detonators using Fulminate of Mercury.

FEB. 6, 1909.

AWFUL
DISASTER
OFF
CAISTER.

EXPLOSIVE-LADEN KETCH BLOWN UP.

SIX TRINITY MEN KILLED.

EYE-WITNESS' THRILLING STORY.

NARROW ESCAPE OF TRINITY STEAMER AND COCKLE LIGHTSHIP.

ONE SURVIVOR—ONE BODY RECOVERED.

OPENING OF THE INQUEST.

Headlines and photographs in *The Yarmouth Mercury* record the tragedy of the Cockle lightship.

I well remember being sent on a Diving and Explosives Course at Portsmouth Naval Base in 1943 soon after being promoted to Second Officer, to prepare me for this wreck-clearing task in future years. I found then that the Navy had discontinued the use of mercury detonators many years before and the Instructor warned me that they were considered obsolete and highly unstable!

There were many occasions when lightships were damaged by collision with passing ships and several were sunk as a result. The list makes sombre reading. Only those sunk are listed here and the records do not mention any loss of life or injuries to crew.

No 5 at the Tongue off Margate in 1877
No 49 at the Kentish Knock off Harwich in 1886
No 9 at the Breaksea off Barry in 1896
No 19 at the Dudgeon off the Wash in 1898
No 21 at the Dover Pier works in 1901
No 41 at the Dover Pier works in 1902
No 28 at the Dudgeon off the Wash in 1902
No 70 at the Morecambe Bay off Fleetwood in 1903
No 57 at the Cross Sand off Great Yarmouth in 1915
No 34 at the English and Welsh Grounds in the Bristol Channel in 1916
No 38 at the Gull off Deal in 1929. Subsequently raised.
No 47 at the Scarweather off Swansea in 1942.

There were other losses in addition to those listed here. Number 30 was struck by a drifting mine at the Corton station off Great Yarmouth in 1916 with the loss of all hands and 19 or 20 other lightships disappeared during World War II due to enemy action. Fortunately that was after most of them had become unmanned stations.

At the Gull station in 1929 there was one life lost as the Master was trapped in his cabin when a ship collided with her in fog. His body was subsequently recovered when the ship was raised. The lightship herself was sold after the last war for use as a yacht clubhouse on the Thames and still exists, although much dilapidated.

A very unusual cause of a lightship sinking occurred, not on station, but while moored in Cowes Harbour prior to a refit in dry dock. The berth chosen for her was fairly shallow and she was allowed to sit on the bottom at low water because it was soft and muddy and should not cause any harm. Such a berth will hold a small ship very firmly by the suction of the mud so it is essential that all portholes are kept closed during the period of low water until the rising tide releases her from that suction.

Unknown light vessel sunk in Cowes harbour

Gull lightship in the early 1900s. She used to mark the western side of the Goodwin sands. Her lantern had to be lowered every day to clean the glazing of the lantern and trim the wicks in the lamps.

As the photograph on page 47 shows, this precaution was not observed and the lightship concerned filled up one night and finished almost on her beam ends!

The worst peacetime accident to a lightship happened on the night of 26th November 1954 when the *South Goodwin* was torn from her moorings during a violent gale and was wrecked on the Goodwin Sands. None of her crew of seven survived and none of their bodies was ever recovered. She was flung broadside on to the sand bank and was already partly full of sand by the time any rescuer was able to board her on the 28th November. Remarkably there was one survivor of the tragedy but he was not a crew member. He was a scientist and a bird watcher who was spending a week on board. He managed to get on deck when the lightship was driven aground and survived by clinging to a boat davit for several hours until rescued at daylight by a helicopter from Manston airfield.

Because of the speed at which the lightship was engulfed and the impossibility of excavating her anchor cable it was not possible to know if she dragged her heavy cable together with the 5-ton anchor attached to it or whether the cable actually parted.

A similar incident happened to the East Goodwin lightship on Sunday 12th November 1961 but fortunately without loss of life. On this occasion she parted her cable about 80 fathoms from the anchor, leaving her to drag the remaining 90 fathoms, of the 170 she was riding to, slowly away from her proper position. Fortunately this took her clear of the sandbank and not on to it.

By the time the Master had decided that there was something amiss and had dropped one of her spare anchors, the Coastguard at Deal had monitored what was happening and alerted the Walmer lifeboat. He also told the North Foreland radio station who began broadcasting a warning to shipping in the Dover Straits and a message also went to the Trinity House Depot at Harwich with the grim news.

South Goodwin lightship which replaced the craft lost in 1954. This later vessel had a helicopter landing pad.

This message was relayed by someone to the news desk at the BBC in London where it was then broadcast to the nation at the close of the Royal Variety programme at 10.00 pm. At that time Trinity House had four of its tenders based at Harwich and one was always 'on call' for just such an emergency. On this occasion it was one called *Vestal* and I was her Commander. A few minutes before the BBC broadcast I had been alerted by the Superintendent to muster my crew at once, to load a new 5-ton anchor and a complete new cable, 270 fathoms of it, and proceed as soon as possible to the aid of the lightship.

This involved calling out a working party to man the shore depot and transport all this massive weight of chain and anchor down to the ship, some four hours work in the middle of the night! The chain consisted of 18 separate lengths, each 15 fathoms long, which the ship would have to shackle together to form one length of new cable.

The weather was absolutely atrocious but we eventually left Harwich about 4.00 am on Monday and battled our way to the Dover straits to wait our chance to put things right. The lightship was almost six miles off station so was not able to exhibit her station signal (her powerful flashing light) and North Foreland radio continued issuing the navigation warning. The lifeboat had been relieved by the one from Ramsgate and she in turn was relieved by the Dover boat later on. This was done as a reassurance to the crew of the lightship who had been considerably shaken at the realisation that they could have been swept on to the Goodwin Sands if the wind had been in a different direction.

The weather was too bad for us to start putting matters right but we were able to anchor on the sheltered side of the Goodwins and to start work at daylight next day, a Tuesday, connecting up all those 18 separate lengths of cable. Each shackle pin had to be separately heated in a portable forge and then each length of chain joined to its neighbour to form the whole anchor cable. Later that day the weather began to moderate and the lifeboat was withdrawn to her station as it was obvious that the lightship was safely riding to her spare anchor.

The next day, Wednesday, was a much better day and we were able to tow the lightship into quieter waters to enable us to transfer the new cable and new anchor to her. Before commencing this tow we had fixed her position and confirmed that she was anchored on the route of a Post Office submarine cable going across to France and was almost certainly hooked on to it. The Post Office had warned me of this and it proved correct. We had to cut the lightship's cable at the 15 fathom shackle and abandon that anchor rather than risk any damage to the submarine one. We were then about halfway through this whole operation.

Early next morning we towed the lightship back to her proper station and anchored her about 300 yards from it. This was to allow us to search for her old anchor and 80 fathoms of cable and recover it so that her new anchor would not be fouled by it. This tedious search by dragging our heavy grapnel through and around her proper position took over five hours, hampered somewhat because in the search we recovered an old aircraft propeller and another very ancient anchor and cable hooked into the one we were seeking.

When we finally recovered the lost cable and 5-ton anchor we found the reason why it had parted. Its links were made from steel rod, one and five-eighth inches in diameter, each one electrically welded to form a solid oval ring. But the broken link had a faulty weld and it had opened up to look like a hook which had finally become unhooked. This link soon found its way back to Trinity House for the inevitable 'inquest' with the chain manufacturer and the result was that Trinity House insisted thereafter that all lightship cable had every link X-rayed to check that each weld was a good one.

The Master of the lightship, Mr W E Harvey, became quite a celebrity as a result of the publicity given to the plight of the lightship. He had been asked several times by the Press over the radio if he wished to abandon his ship, but quite rightly refused. As a result he subsequently received a great many letters of congratulation and was also awarded the B.E.M in the Queen's Birthday Honours for 1962. He was also invited to open the 1962 International Boat Show at Olympia and was much admired for the way he carried out this special function.

An earlier wooden lightship at the East Goodwin station also hit the headlines, in 1898, but for quite a different reason. Marconi, the pioneer of wireless telegraphy, conducted some of his early experiments between that lightship and his base at North Foreland over a period of two years. He spent a week on board on one occasion and sent a message to the Prince of Wales by morse. This obviously pleased the

Prince since he responded by sending every member of the crew a ½lb of tobacco.

At some stage of the experiments the lightship was run into by a large four-masted ship and was quite badly damaged. A message was then sent by radio telegraphy for assistance and the lightship was taken in for repairs. Apparently this was the first occasion in the world that a distress signal was sent from any ship by wireless This historic event apparently caused a boom in the shares of the Marconi Company when people realised the far reaching possibilities of such an invention.

One of the most important duties that a lightship Master had was the care of his anchor cable. A landsman might think that once a ship was safely anchored all would remain secure. In the case of a ship at anchor for only a day or two, perhaps waiting outside a port for a berth to be cleared, this could be quite true, but not for a lightship.

In her case she would be on station for up to three years or even longer and it was vital to ensure that the anchor remained firmly embedded in the sea-bed and that the cable did not become wrapped around it at each turn of the tide. There were no laid down rules about this for each station was different, for example, in depth of water, strength of tide and the amount of shelter from the sand bank she might be marking. The rule of thumb about how much cable to let out was six times the depth of water for fair weather but considerably more if it was rough. This extra length had to be hove in after the storm so that it did not become fouled—the sailors' term for 'tangled up'. This did happen on a number of occasions and had to be cleared by one of the tenders. A most time-consuming job if the bunch of cable was a large one.

I recall just such a job at the *Seven Stones* lightship off Land's End which took a whole day to clear. We had to moor alongside the lightship and slip her cable to our ship. The capstan could only heave in about half the cable before the weight of the 4 ton anchor, plus the huge bunch of cable wound round it was too heavy for it. The depth of water at this station was over 40 fathoms. We then had to use the ship's main derrick to recover the whole mass and land it on our deck, where it had to be cut apart to clear it and then reconnected before laying it all out again.

When powered windlasses began to be introduced to lightships between the two wars the work of hauling in cable and stowing it in the chain locker became much easier. Prior to this improvement all windlasses on lightships were manual and the chain lockers were underneath the crew's quarters. That was just a single open space with a hammock for each man and a wooden table with two benches. When the cable had to be attended to all hands were required, everything had to be lashed up and stowed to make room for the hatches to be lifted and to keep their personal gear free from the rust and dirt flying about when the cable was paid out. There were quite a number of these old ships still in use after World War II much to the consternation of new recruits to the lightship Service who expected something better!

The foredeck of *Seven Stones* light vessel showing the main anchor cable in the centre and her two spare cables at each side. They are connected to her spare anchors which are housed in the bays on either side of her bow.

One major inconvenience for the crews of some lightships was a submarine bell which worked in conjunction with her fog signal. This bell hung over the side about six or seven feet below the waterline, about level with the sleeping quarters. It was designed to be heard by an approaching ship that would have to carry an underwater listening device known as a hydrophone. By careful monitoring of consecutive fog signals through the air and bell signals through the water one should be able to calculate how far away the lightship might be, but I have no idea now effective it was.

The bell was later replaced by an oscillator which sounded a shrill piercing signal underwater instead. When the weather was bad and the wind was against the tide causing the ship to roll heavily, it also caused either the bell or the oscillator to bump heavily against the hull. They both weighed about five hundredweight so sleep was badly affected. Unfortunately this 'slight' inconvenience for the crew was not considered sufficient to warrant any extra pay for them as the fog signal did. When I joined the Service just before the war the listening device was still fitted in the *Alert* but the whole underwater system was about to be discontinued.

It is over 100 years since telephone and telegraphic communication were brought into use and it is interesting to note that Trinity House was in the very forefront of its use at sea. A Royal Commission on Electrical Communication in 1892 decided to experiment with setting up links with H M Coastguard, the Lifeboat Service and the Lighthouse Service. Trinity House later recommended that Lightships and possibly Rock Lighthouses should also be included. The intention was of course to speed communication between these services when lives were in danger at sea.

The experiment began in 1894 by linking the Sunk lightship off Walton in Essex to the shore by telegraphic cable and when this was a proven success it was extended to the Kentish Knock in the Thames entrance, the North Goodwin off Ramsgate, The Shipwash off Orfordness and the Haisborough off the Norfolk coast. All these five Lightships were successfully equipped by the turn of the century, but I do not think any others ever had such equipment as they would have been moored in deeper water, making the telegraphic cable too vulnerable.

The major problem of course was to get the electric cable into the lightship and keep it clear of her anchor and cable lying on the sea bed. This was accomplished by laying out two anchors and two cables, one up-tide and one down-tide. These were joined with a large swivel at the lightship's position and her anchor cable was connected to it as well so that she could hold it about six fathoms off the sea bed. The swivel had a hole in the top of it and the electric cable from the shore was passed up through it and in to the lightship. It was a very successful arrangement.

Some of the lightships were in very exposed positions and in order to ensure their safety, and that of the electric cable, they were given four anchors each with a separate cable and all connected to the large swivel. These four arms were laid at right angles to the lightship's position. All these cables were 210 fathoms long and it was a mammoth operation involving two of the tenders to lay them out in one day.

The first four-arm mooring ever laid by Trinity House was at the Tongue station off Margate in 1892, the same year that the Royal Commission was instituted. So it would appear that the work at the Tongue was almost certainly done as an experiment. These multi-arm moorings remained in use until 1923 when radio-telephony was introduced to the Service. The lightships then reverted to single moorings. The electric cable was, of course, laid out between the lightship and the shore by a Post Office telegraph cable ship.

In 1940 several of these lightships were again fitted with four-arm moorings and were provided with submarine telephone cables for wartime security purposes but the nature of hostilities soon made it necessary for those ships to be withdrawn.

Some time in the late 1960s Trinity House learned of an American development of a very large buoy for use in deep water. The Engineer's department at Trinity House sent some of their personnel to the U.S.A. to examine it and eventually the idea was adopted for use in our coastal waters. The device was called a 'Lanby'. This name stood for Large Automated Navigational Buoy although that name was rarely used. The buoy was really huge, having a diameter of 40 feet with a light tower on it standing 40 feet above the sea.

L.A.N.B.Y. being brought to Blackwall workshops for modification.
(photos: J. Ridgeon)

Trinity House bought five or six of these huge navigational aids but all have now been withdrawn from service. I think the main reason for that is because they were so expensive to buy and to maintain. Several of them were put out of action by collision with a large ship which was often not reported, leaving Trinity House to foot the bill. One or two of them actually had their hulls sliced open and needed urgent attention in dry dock. Their hulls contained several watertight compartments to keep them afloat in just such an emergency.

The photographs show one of these monsters after repair at Blackwall workshops and being put back into the water by a huge floating crane. That was on hire from the Port of London Authority and was a very costly piece of equipment.

The final photograph in this chapter shows an even more unusual task which was given to one of our ships called *Beacon*, rather appropriately. Prior to the last war there were a number of large beacons in the Thames Estuary, over a dozen I believe. They were sunk into various sand banks to mark these shallow areas and carried a very large, distinctive, topmark to identify them. This was on the top of a stout wooden mast which in turn was wedged firmly into a two-foot wide steel tube sunk in the sand, about 25 or 30 feet long.

When the war started it was decided to remove these topmarks to ensure that any low flying enemy aircraft would not be helped to find their way too easily to Sheerness, Chatham or Southend.

After the war these beacons were gradually re-instated when a tender had a couple of days to spare and this particular operation was photographed by a low flying aircraft. The working party, having installed a new mast in the tube and wedged it into place, are waiting for the tender to edge close enough to put the large wooden topmark in place on the top of the mast using the ship's derrick. It was quite a delicate manoeuvre.

This was a welcome job as all members of the working party earned a small bonus—exept one. He was the supervising officer standing behind the coxswain of the launch, wearing a uniform cap and answering to the name of Tarrant.

This L.A.N.B.Y., of a slightly different design, was stationed in Morecambe Bay. A tug tows it out to one of the Trinity House tenders, with her boat in attendance.

(photo: J. Ridgeon)

An example of one of the little known jobs undertaken by a Trinity House crew: reinstating a beacon.

Chapter 5

The Lighthouse Service

This branch of the Trinity House Service is probably the best known since so many of the stations have such a high profile for the news media. A few of the land-based ones may not attract much attention except from holidaymakers in the near vicinity but the large towers such as Eddystone, Longships and Bishop Rock have often been in the news.

In particular Bishop Rock attracted worldwide attention at Christmas 1946 when the BBC arranged a Round the World link-up by radio from there before the King's speech on Christmas Day. The two BBC men, Edward Ward the link man and commentator, and Stanley Coombs the engineer, were landed on the station the day before and expected to be taken off again on Boxing Day. In the event they were marooned there for 28 days by bad weather and attracted attention almost daily throughout January. Whenever they made a broadcast the keepers had to rig up a make-shift tent of blankets in their living room to deaden the hollow sound of the tower.

This episode in the history of Bishop Rock happened long before helicopters were introduced into the lighthouse story. It increased the public's awareness of the rigorous and spartan life of a lighthouse keeper and prompted quite a flood of sympathetic letters as a result.

This station is built on an isolated pinnacle of rock on the extreme outer limit of the Isles of Scilly and is exposed to the full force of the Atlantic storms. The top of this pinnacle is only 153 feet long by 52 feet broad and rises 120 feet sheer and steep from the sea bed. An attempt was begun in 1847 to build a lighthouse using separate iron columns to allow the heavy seas to wash through them. The work was almost completed in February 1850 when it was completely destroyed by a violent storm. Fortunately there was no loss of life.

Trinity House then decided to build a granite tower and this work, begun in 1851, was completed in 1858. It was not altogether satisfactory and had to be strengthened by various means over the next twenty years because some of the blocks had pieces of granite split away by the force of the sea. The vibration of the tower in storm conditions could cause articles to be shaken off the shelves and some of the prisms of the lighting apparatus to be fractured.

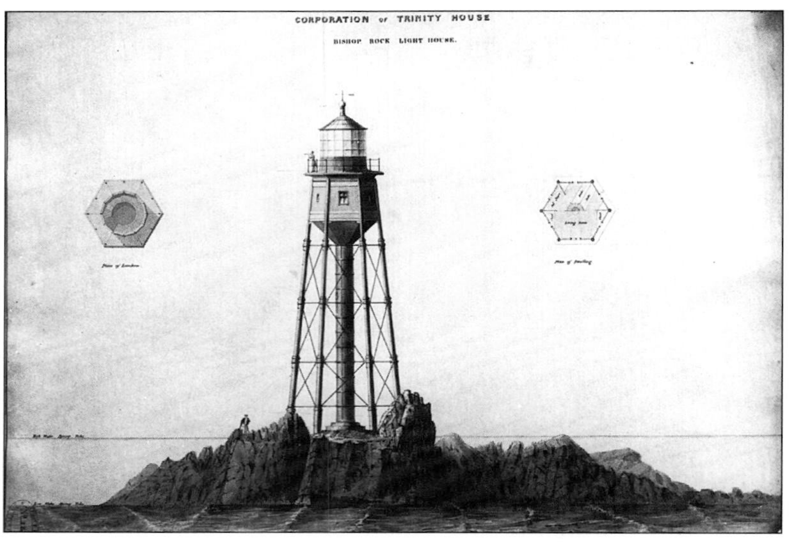

The first tower built at Bishop Rock, destroyed by a violent gale before the light was installed.

Eventually it was decided to carry out major improvements to the tower by giving it a complete outer casing of masonry blocks dovetailed to each other and into the original tower. The building was also heightened and given four new rooms. This entailed the removal of the lantern and lighting apparatus, the provision of a temporary lantern on a long mast until completion of the work and the re-instatement of these items afterwards. This work was begun in 1882 and finished in October 1887.

The man who master-minded this really stupendous work from its beginning in 1847 was Nicholas Douglass, born in 1798, assisted by his son James Nicholas Douglass born in 1826. James was later knighted after the successful conclusion of his work in building the present Eddystone Lighthouse in 1882.

One great improvement to the Bishop Rock tower, learned from experience gained at the Eddystone, was the construction of a new landing platform around the base of the tower. This has a vertical side instead of the curved one of the original tower which it now encases. James Douglass had given careful thought as to why heavy seas at the

The second tower at Bishop Rock being stengthened and heightened by adding a 'jacket' around it.

(photo: Gibson, St Mary's)

old Eddystone tower, which was built by Smeaton, would so easily envelop it in bad weather. He concluded that if he built the new Eddystone with the landing platform having vertical sides and not curved ones this would have the effect of repelling the waves rather than assisting them to shoot upwards as Smeaton's tower did. Experience after the Eddystone one was completed in 1882 showed how correct he was and this has been shown again at the Bishop.

One unfortunate result of this design however has been to persuade some people that this platform was actually a coffer dam and that the two towers built on the Bishop were actually built inside it. This is quite erroneous. The pinnacle on which it stands is simply not big enough to allow such a thing to be built even if the sea had allowed it to be done.

A coffer dam was certainly used at the commencement of James Douglass' tower at Eddystone because he found a level section of the reef which never quite uncovered at low water and the dam was necessary to lay the first three or four courses inside it before they were high enough to be above the low water mark. The dam, which is built of granite blocks, as the tower is also, is still around the base and can be seen at low water. It took one year just to build this coffer dam before the tower could be started.

One item of interest concerning the first stone tower at Bishop Rock clearly illustrates the difficulty the builders had. The work started in 1851 and the lowest stone was eventually laid one foot below low water spring tide because this was necessary to get the greatest possible diameter of the base. However this particular stone was not actually laid until the end of 1852 by which time several courses of blocks had already been fixed above that level.

The official narrative of the work, written by William Tregarthen Douglass, son of Sir James, indicates that all the work of lifting and fixing the stones for the first tower was entirely done by hand. The stones themselves were conveyed by barges towed from the work yard on St Mary's Island. When the second tower was built around the first one, the workforce was assisted by a steam winch on the deck of the steamer Hercules. She belonged to Trinity House and had previously been used in the construction of the fourth Eddystone tower by James Douglass.

Bishop's Rock lighthouse, complete with helipad.
(photo: Gibson, St Mary's)

Longships Lighthouse, some years before the fitting of a helipad. The very dirty streak below the middle window was caused by the kitchen waste tipped out of the kitchen window. The smaller streak above was caused by the emptying of chamber pots.

Trinity House built seven of these isolated tower lighthouses totally surrounded by sea. They were the Smalls (in the Irish Sea), Longships and Wolf Rock off Lands End, Bishop Rock, Eddystone off Plymouth, Hanois off Guernsey and Beachy Head near Eastbourne. All were similar in appearance but some were a little shorter than the Bishop Rock which is 168 feet to the helipad above the lantern. There were a number of other lighthouses built on various islands around the coast and plenty of others built on the mainland, all of them built with more room inside and a less spartan appearance. All the seven tower lights were originally built with a proper toilet in them and a soil pipe leading down into the sea through the foundations. Unfortunately they all suffered from being damaged by the sea and the enormous pressure exerted by heavy waves during storms. The soil pipes were usually combined with the waste pipe from the kitchen and there were unpleasant incidents when the contents of the pipe sometimes hit the ceiling. Long before I first saw the inside of a lighthouse these toilets had been abandoned and the soil pipes sealed in favour of a chemical toilet which was situated in the lantern room.

New keepers quickly learned which was the windward side when using the 'bucket and chuck it' method and found a hidden meaning in the old phrase 'getting your own back'!

When the Equal Opportunities Act opened up the possibility of having women as lighthouse keepers it was not difficult to deter them by mentioning this problem. There was also the fact that all hands on a tower light slept in bunks in one room. These were curved of course to follow the shape of the room and were known as 'banana bunks'. A tall man was never able to sleep comfortably in one of them.

The washing facilities in these towers were also very spartan, consisting of one sink in the kitchen with cold water from a tank above it. Hot water was provided by a large kettle on the stove. If a man wanted a bath he used a bucket, standing in it—one foot at a time—and of course having to clear up the inevitable mess on the deck. All the floors in these places were of stone or slate, so were cold to walk on despite a meagre covering of mats.

These towers all suffered with the problem of condensation on the walls which were all quite cold. Above the kitchen level it was not too bad because of the warmth rising from the stove, but below that the walls would sometimes stream with water. This was a particular problem after a period of dry and bright weather followed by a warm front with a mild south west wind. This could result in the lower half running with condensation.

There were no refrigerators in lighthouses until after 1950 so the men developed all kinds of ideas to keep food fresh until the next relief. Salted fish and salt meat was popular of course and some men would preserve fresh meat by cooking it and sealing it with mutton fat in jars. Catching fish in fine weather was sometimes possible but one always had the difficulty of getting the hook to the outside of the rocks where the fish were.

The really ingenious method was kite fishing from the lantern gallery. The kite was a large one, 5 or 6 feet tall and usually made by the keeper. It needed a very long tail which carried the baited hook as far out as possible. It needed skill, and a bit of strength, to fly the kite out rather than up, and low enough to keep the bait submerged. When a fish was hooked the extra weight, perhaps 3 or 4 pounds, would make the kite shoot up and lift the catch quite high.

More skill was then needed to play the kite so that a man could grab the line, remove the fish and still keep it flying ready for the next cast. It was said that a really skilled fisherman could bring the kite in so that the fish would be hanging just level with the kitchen window several floors below. A quick tap on the chimney flue that came up beside the lantern would alert the cook of the day to reach out of the window and retrieve the fresh supply. A real fisherman's tale!

The window referred to above was quite different from one seen in a house ashore. In a tower lighthouse the wall would be about 2 feet thick at the top and up to 8 feet thick at the bottom. So all windows were fitted on the outer end of a small tunnel and flush with the outer wall face. The frames were made of gun metal about one inch thick with an opening section of similar thickness carrying thick glass.

There was an amusing incident concerning the Bishop Rock in 1951. The keepers all lived in Service cottages on St Mary's Island and one possessed a bicycle. He decided to take it off to the tower on his next turn of duty in order to strip it down for overhaul.

Before he could begin this work the local tender arrived to deliver coal, oil and water and it was necessary to hang the machine outside the tower for most of the day and the next to keep it clear of the work. As usual when the tender worked at this station the local boatmen brought boatloads of visitors to watch the proceedings and the story of the mad keeper who kept his bike on the lighthouse was soon relayed all over the islands!

On another occasion an inflatable life-size dummy of a female was taken off to the lighthouse and the keeper concerned had great fun pretending to cuddle and kiss 'her' in the doorway for the benefit of the visitors outside. 'She' was apparently a surprise present from his wife.

The kite which was used for fishing had another use at Bishop Rock as the local boatmen also brought out the keeper's mail and daily papers. With a boatload of sightseers it was not possible to get close enough to hand these up to the men so they used the kite to retrieve them which created great interest for the passengers.

Before the introduction of helicopters to the Service all entry to a tower lighthouse was via two heavy metal doors at the bottom of the habitable section. Below this was a flight of bronze steps outside, let into the solid section of it. These doors are at least an inch thick and are fitted with heavy bolts top and bottom plus two heavy bars set at an angle on the inside as strong backs to prevent any heavy seas from breaking them down.

The doors fitted to the Bishop Rock tower have remained intact since 1887 and they always seemed quite impregnable, but one must never trust the sea. Incredible as it sounds, during a violent storm early in 1994 both doors were battered down and completely smashed.

It was known at the time that a merchant ship carrying a deck cargo of very heavy timber had lost a large amount of it when in the vicinity of the Isles of Scilly. It was evident that some of these tree trunks had been flung repeatedly against the lighthouse doors until they collapsed. They are now prime exhibits in the Trinity House Museum at Penzance.

All the other lighthouses built by Trinity House have an equally interesting history. The most famous one being the Eddystone light lying some 8 miles out from Rame Head at the entrance to Plymouth Sound. There were four separate towers built here between 1698 and

1882. The first one, built by Henry Winstanley had to be radically strengthened and heightened after the first winter so it is usually considered that the total was really five. Winstanley had no encouragement at all from The Elder Brethren as they considered that it was an impossible task.

That strengthened tower survived until 1703 when it was swept away in the worst storm ever known in England. Winstanley himself, plus some workmen, were on board and, together with the three lighthouse keepers everyone was lost. These keepers were the first ever to be lost from their station. The third tower, built of wood by John Rudyerd in 1709 survived for 47 years before it caught fire and was destroyed. The senior keeper is still remembered today because he swallowed a large piece of molten lead running off the roof while he was fighting the fire. The gruesome relic was found in his stomach after his death and is still preserved in Edinburgh at the National Museum of Scotland.

'Smeaton's Eddystone Lighthouse' by William Gibbons.
(Plymouth City Museums and Art Gallery)

The present Eddystone tower nearing completion in 1881.
(photo: Plymouth Library)

The fourth tower was built by John Smeaton between 1756 and 1759 and lasted for 127 years until the rock on which it stood showed signs of cracking. It was commemorated after 100 years use by the engraving of a tiny lighthouse at the feet of Britannia on the back of the old penny then in use. It was finally taken down and re-erected on Plymouth Hoe because the townspeople could not bear to see it abandoned.

By then it had been replaced by the present tower, built by James Douglass in 1882 and still in use. He was afterwards knighted for his work. The full story of these works is well told by Fred Majdalany in his book *The Red Rocks of Eddystone* (Longman 1959).

Wolf Rock, 1978.

The Wolf Rock lighthouse is another magnificent example of Victorian engineering. It was built between 1862 and 1870 about 8 miles south west of Lands End with no loss of life or even any serious injury. The rock had been a veritable graveyard for ships before then and indeed is the resting place for a German submarine which drove on to it during the last war. Part of her crew were rescued by a British destroyer before she finally went down. Before this lighthouse was built Trinity House had managed to erect an unlighted beacon on the rock after several failed attempts. This one consisted of a large cast-iron cone with a mast carrying a topmark. When Douglass built the lighthouse he incorporated the cone into the landing area as a refuge for men against sudden big waves when working on the landing.

Douglas Hague's reconstruction diagram of the first Smalls Lighthouse.
(from *Lighthouses, their Architectural, History and Archaeology)*

As previously mentioned, this lighthouse was the first one in the world to be equipped with a helicopter landing platform mounted above the lantern. Trinity House is justly proud of this achievement which has been copied by many other countries.

The Smalls lighthouse is another rock tower worthy of note. It is built on a reef of that name about 22 miles WSW from St David's Head in Wales. The first tower here was built of wood and again it was not considered a practical proposition by Trinity House and was built privately.

It was constructed by a man named Henry Whiteside at the instigation of a Mr Philips who owned the reef and was prepared to pay the cost of the undertaking. He was inspired, of course, by the success of Winstanley's lighthouse at Eddystone.

Henry Whiteside was a surprising choice for the job as he was a Musical Instrument Maker and only just 26 years old when he was given it. He started work in 1772 from a base at Solva, a small port on the Welsh coast. He built the tower with eight massive wooden pillars after experimenting with iron ones which were not satisfactory. On top of the piles he built a room for the light keepers with a second room above to house the lantern. The tower was finished in 1776 and was very successful. It survived until James Douglass built the present granite tower which was finished in 1861 when the old one was removed. There are stumps of the original piles still to be seen embedded in the rock.

The base of the Smalls Lighthouse, 1972, where stumps are the remains of the first lighthouse.

Lighthouses are funded by Light Dues which are levied on ships that have passed their station and are collected by H M Customs when the ship arrives in port. The Smalls is renowned as having been the most lucrative lighthouse in the world. This was in the days when most of them were privately owned and the increase of shipping when Britain was a great trading nation enabled these owners to receive quite enormous amounts of revenue.

In 1836 an Act of Parliament allowed these private owners to be bought out and Trinity House to take over control of them. It was a long and costly procedure and the story can be found in Douglas Hague and Rosemary Christie's book, *Lighthouses* (Gomer Press, 1975). Each private lighthouse had to be bought out for an agreed sum and for the Smalls lighthouse this was £170,142. This however was by no means the biggest sum paid to a lighthouse owner. By 1841 the last private lighthouse was the Skerries which lies off the north west coast of Anglesey on a small island. The original owner was Morgan Jones who died in 1826 and his nephew inherited the property. For five years following the Act of 1836 he turned down successive offers of £260,000, £350,000 and £399,500. He died in 1841 and his executors insisted on having a jury to agree the settlement figure. This was set at £444,984 11s 3d, and is the highest compensation ever paid for one lighthouse. The total sum paid out by Trinity House to buy out the last ten private lighthouses was £1,182,546.

The Longships lighthouse off Lands End is another one with an interesting history and there have been two towers on the same site. The first one was built by a Lieutenant Henry Smith under a licence granted by Trinity House. It was completed in 1795 and he was to pay a rent of £100 per year for 50 years while at the same time collecting Light Dues for the ships which had passed it. Soon afterwards he was declared incapable of managing the station and Trinity House took it over.

The tower was only 40 feet tall and stood on the highest part of the rock 40 feet above sea level. In consequence its light was often obscured by heavy seas breaking over it and causing damage on several occasions. Eventually it was decided to build a bigger tower, which was done between 1870 and 1873 and this was erected alongside the first one which was afterwards demolished. The decision to replace it was a

Longships Lighthouse during re-modernisation work.
(photo: BOC Gases)

timely one, as in 1874 the rock on which it had been standing split away and slid into the sea.

The present Beachy Head lighthouse is another well known tower and is interesting because it is the second one built to mark that headland and the first one is still standing. This was built in 1831 and is called Belle Tout. It probably got that name from an Anglo Saxon word 'totian' meaning 'to peep'. Unfortunately it was built on the top of the cliff which turned out to be the completely wrong place for it! It was so high and the cliff-top attracted so much low cloud that the light was obscured far more than it was visible. Eventually Trinity House was prevailed upon to build the present tower at the foot of the cliffs in 1902, about 200 yards out from the base. The work was done from the top of the cliff by means of an aerial ropeway to a temporary platform erected beside the site of the new tower.

Beachy Head Lighthouse, at the foot of the cliffs.

(photo: Abreas Köllner)

This was not the only lighthouse to have been erected in the wrong place. The Needles, on the Isle of Wight, also has that distinction. It was first built early in the 1800s on the top of the cliffs, well above its present position, where it, too, suffered from low cloud. In 1859 it was re-designed and built on its present site at the base of the chalk cliffs.

A third station to have had this shortcoming was the first Lundy Island lighthouse built in 1819 on that island's western side. It was put on the highest point, called Beacon Hill, nearly 500 feet above the sea and with an 80 foot tower. It, too, was frequently obscured by fog or low cloud which rendered it useless on those occasions.

About 20 years after its erection Trinity House added a fog signal which consisted of two 18-pounder cannon dating back to the reign of William IV. The noise when they were fired could be heard on the Cornish coast some 15 miles away and of course it was a great inconvenience to the families of the keepers living at the station. As a result Trinity House built a fog signal station in about 1860 which was half a mile away from the lighthouse with two cottages for the fog signal keepers.

A Trinity House Gunner lighting a signal rocket, about 1875.
The 18-pounder cannon dates from the reign of William IV.
(Photo: Myrtle Langham)

Trinity House Gunners with their families outside the Battery Cottages, about 1875.
(Photo: Myrtle Langham)

In the late 1890s Trinity House built two new lighthouses at the north and south ends of the island, closer to sea level, and the earlier tower was abandoned. It is still standing and used infrequently by bird watchers, but the fog signal station is much decayed although I believe the two cannon are still surviving.

In addition to those historic stone lighthouses built to last for centuries there was another class of lighthouse which is almost non-existent around our shore. These were pile lighthouses and were mostly designed for use in rivers and their estuaries where they were installed in sand banks and sometimes in mud banks.

The most well known ones are the four built in the lower reaches of the Thames and in its estuary. They were introduced when Alexander Mitchell, an Irish engineer invented the cast iron screw pile. James Walker was the Trinity House engineer who built them and two of these are illustrated here. The Mucking lighthouse in the Mucking Bight (a bend in the river just below Gravesend) and the Chapman lighthouse in the lower reach of the Thames.

The third one shown here is still standing and is one of a pair on the shore line at Dovercourt. This pair was erected to give a 'leading line' into Harwich entrance. The two others in the Thames estuary marking dangerous sand banks also no longer exist.

The Chapman lighthouse in the Lower Reach of the river Thames.
She was one of five Pile Lighthouse between the Thames and Walton-on-Naze, Essex.
All have gone now.

One of several Pile lighthouses used in the Thames estuary.
This one was in the Mucking Bight just below Gravesend, long since gone.

Lighthouse and beach, Dovercourt

Chapter 6

The Lighthouse Relief

The advent of helicopters into the Service quite transformed the work of 'reliefs' either for lighthouses or lightships. It was welcomed by all personnel in the 'afloat' services who little realised that it was the beginning of the end for most of their jobs.

The whole learning process was quite prolonged. All the tenders and the lightships had to be fitted with a landing platform, known as a helideck, as did the tower lighthouses. The island lighthouses, too, needed a level landing space, known as a helipad.

A proper drill had to be devised and learned, so that the helicopter crew and all hands on the tenders and stations knew exactly what to do. Some of the work was quite new to the helicopter personnel, especially the landing on a moving platform on the tenders and lightships.

With the coming of helicopters entry to the tower lighthouses is now very much easier. Each of the helidecks are above the lantern which has been altered so that its top is level and not dome shaped. When keepers were still there, as soon as the helicopter landed the incoming men would leap out, lift one of the hinged traps in the helideck and begin lowering down their boxes of provisions and other stores on to the gallery around the lantern. The outgoing keepers would have their boxes and suitcases all ready to go into the helicopter and the whole relief would only take two or three minutes to complete. The helicopter blades remained turning the whole time.

Compared with the old routine of landing from a boat which might easily take one or two hours it seemed unbelievable to people used to the old method. Now there is no relief at all on rock stations or lightships and only a few land stations are still manned. They too will be deserted before the end of the century.

The helicopter is still needed for routine maintenance and inspections. Every automated station is constantly monitored every few seconds and the signal is transmitted to the controlling shore station which acts on the information received. Eventually these shore stations too will be automated and unmanned and the signals from all stations will then be routed to the main control point in the Trinity House depot at Harwich who will arrange for the necessary action in the event of a fault.

The stations still need to be supplied with oil and water and both commodities are flown out by the helicopter in underslung rubber bags holding 100 gallons each. Both commodities are landed on the helideck and the bags are connected by flexible pipes to the tanks in the tower. Water is still needed in the event that engineers have to stay on the station for several days work overhauling or repairing engine faults.

Oil and fresh water are delivered to lighthouses in 100-gallon portolite tanks carried underslung by the Trinity House helicopter.

In previous times these items were supplied by the lighthouse tender, water in 9 gallon wooden casks, oil in 5 gallon drums. All had to be separately slung and winched by hand crane on to the lighthouse landing. They were then re-slung in some cases, in order to get them up into the tower to be emptied. All done by a working party from the tender and the assistance of the keepers.

Stella anchored close in to shore to enable oil and water hoses to be passed ashore at Round Island.

After World War II there was an influx of new ideas into the Service, one of which was the introduction in about 1952 of rubber hoses and small portable pumps to transfer oil and water from tanks carried in the ship's boats to some of the lighthouses. This made a considerable difference to the work load. Sacks of coal still went up by hand winch as did the heavy store boxes containing the keepers food and clothing. The established routine was to stock up the lighthouses and lightvessels in the autumn with as much of these necessities as they could hold. Then, hopefully, a winter relief would not be quite such a protracted job. In the early days of the Lighthouse Service all this work was done by pulling boat. The introduction of motor boats to the tenders was a slow process and did not commence until almost the 1930s because they were considered insufficiently reliable for work at lighthouses. This was 200 years after the Nore lightship was laid and 230 after the first Eddystone relief. This meant that all Trinity House crews were highly proficient in boat work. They took a great pride in their skill and still do so.

This was well illustrated by a magazine article written by a man named Hubert Hudson. He was a Second Officer in the tenders some 90 years ago and resigned just prior to World War I to become the Navigating Officer on the *Endurance* when Shackleton made his famous, but ill-fated Antarctic voyage in 1914 to 1916. Hudson was in charge of one of the boats after *Endurance* was abandoned and subsequently wrote a long article for the Nautical Magazine in the 1920s. In this he paid a glowing tribute to the experience he gained in boat handling during his time in the Trinity House Service which stood him in such good stead for the Antarctic ordeal.

In those early days of rock lighthouses it was quite a frequent occurrence for those isolated stations off the Cornish coast to suffer

The Cutter *Joy*, built at Cowes in 1865, having completed the provisioning of the Needles Lighthouse, is about to start the long haul back to her home port of Yarmouth against a strong north-easterly wind.

(from an original painting by Peter Leath, 'Home for Supper') delayed reliefs. In fact they had their own 'cycle' of relief dates as a result. Whereas those stations off the Welsh coast and in the North Sea had a regular 28 days between reliefs because their bad weather conditions were not too prolonged, the Cornish stations had a 29 day cycle to take account of the very long delays they experienced.

The 29 days started on the day that the relief was actually accomplished and the next relief fell due 28 days after a man stepped ashore. This made life very difficult for the man and his family as no holiday arrangements could be made until he was actually ashore. Delays of 7 or 10 days were nothing unusual in winter time and many longer ones are well documented.

While researching for this book I came across an old notebook which contained details of life on the Wolf Rock as far back as 1888. One particularly poignant entry is dated 19th December 1910 and records '*Mermaid* passed west 9.30 am no relief here since October'. (*Mermaid* was the Trinity House tender based at Penzance.) It was followed by a rather sad poem composed by the keeper which could have been equally applicable on a hundred other occasions :

Where is the gallant *Mermaid* now?
Why, safe in dock moored stern and bow.
Her sailors clustered round the mast
Await the order 'keep all fast'.
We watch and spy and wonder why
The gallant ship does not draw nigh.

She cannot come, they've closed the dock,
There's too much sea around the rock.
The sky is looking very dirty
Barometer has dropped to thirty.
The bay will soon be white with foam
So give it up and all go home.

While we poor beggars on the Rock
Have nought to eat but tough salt hock,
Hard tack, stale cakes and mouldy cheese,
'Ramornie' brand hashed up with peas.

(I believe Ramornie brand was corned beef.)

A finer day when relief *did* come to Wolf Rock.
(photo: Norman Fitkin)

There are several other interesting entries, eg :

Feb 10th 1910	'Sea swept over lantern, smashed ladder and started some glazing.' (The ladder was kept lashed on the lantern gallery for use when cleaning the windows.)
Dec 16th 1910	'Heavy sea washing over lantern, smashed exhaust pipe.' (Presumably the galley stove pipe.)
Dec 17th 1924 to Jan 5th 1925	'Very heavy seas going over top of lantern.'

There are numerous other entries regarding wreckage going past the station and of ships passing with damage or bad list after stormy weather. There is also one cheerful entry on 17th February 1927. This records the gift of a two valve wireless set from the Missions to Seamen, given by a Miss Hassard of Lynmouth. The writer adds, 'It has made life a pleasure now.'

The crew of a rock lighthouse was always four men, with three on duty together. Originally they served eight weeks on duty and four ashore. There was also a small group of Supernumerary keepers available to keep the station manned with three men at all times. That routine was altered in the 1970s when Trinity House finally agreed to the keepers' request for a four weeks 'on' and four weeks 'off' routine. I believe it was first requested more than 50 years earlier! There used to be a saying in the Service 'the Mills of God grind slowly but they are like lightning compared with the Mills of Trinity House'!

The very first routine for keepers on a rock lighthouse was at the first Eddystone light in 1698. Only four men were employed and their routine was six weeks on station and two weeks off.

When Smeaton built the third tower at this station in 1759 it is recorded that the keepers' wages were £25 per annum. This was said to be considerably more than a country labourer earned. According to the Central Statistical Office £1 in 1759 would equate to £76 today, so their wages were equivalent to £1,785 per annum in 1998. Fortunately the rates of pay increased over the years although they were always rather poor. In 1935 pay for a junior keeper on appointment was just £7 1s 5d per month. At today's values that would be about £2,890 per annum.

The good seamanship of the tender crews has already been mentioned but nevertheless over a period of more than 200 years of difficult boat work there have been several bad accidents. The Eddystone was the scene of one of these when the *Vestal* was delivering stores there early in 1940. The weather was quite reasonable for the task and the motor boat went in with eight men on board and some stores but was swamped by a sudden large and unexpected wave while mooring up. She was quite unmanageable and sank almost at once throwing everyone into the sea. *Vestal* launched a second boat under oars as soon as the accident was observed but could only recover one man barely alive and no one else. Sadly, he only survived in hospital for about ten days.

Another bad accident happened in Cowes harbour several years after World War II. The ship's boat was ferrying men and materials from the Trinity depot there to the relief ship in Cowes Roads when it was suddenly swamped as she cleared the entrance and met a head sea. She was loaded with coal for the light vessels and other stores and sank immediately, trapping four men under the steel canopy who were all drowned.

A similar accident occurred at the Smalls lighthouse in the 1920s to a pulling boat. This station has a channel through the rocks to the landing place and on this occasion the boat was swamped by a wave coming over the rock and sank alongside the landing. Fortunately all the men were saved but all items of stores and luggage of the men going on duty were lost.

Just over 150 years ago on 14th July 1843 there was another sad accident when the first *Vestal* ran down her own boat and drowned two of the Elder Brethren. At the time the *Vestal* had the Deputy Master and the inspecting Committee on board, having visited the Longships lighthouse and the Isles of Scilly. The two men drowned, Captain Drew and Captain Jenkin Jones were to have landed by pulling boat near to the proposed site for the Trevose lighthouse near Padstow to carry out a survey, but it was too rough to land. They returned to the ship where sadly the boat was caught under the ship's bow and capsized. It was

Warden, a typical working motor boat as carried by all Trinity House Ships since the 1930s—about to be launched to carry out a relief operation.
(photo: Larkin bros.)

manned by eight seamen and fortunately all were saved. The bodies of the two elder Brethren were recovered and landed at Bristol.

The *Vestal* had earlier delivered oil and stores to the Longships lighthouse and probably St Mary's lighthouse on that island. This may surprise some readers since this would seem to be unlikely tasks for the Elder Brethren's committee ship to engage in. But in the Victorian era of stage coaches and early railways it was accepted routine for the inspecting ship to leave London fully loaded with stores for delivery to any lighthouse being visited. The Brethren were mostly ex Masters of Merchant ships so would have considered it a proper use for their ship.

There is still in existence a most interesting note book listing all kinds of unlikely anchorages used by our ships when attending to this task of delivering stores at some of the South Coast lighthouses. In the days of pulling boats it was of course essential to anchor your ship as close to the shore station or any rock lighthouse, in safety, as was possible and to have written advice from previous Captains of the tenders was invaluable. There is even an entry in it which tells the Captain where to land the inspecting Committee a mile or two from the Trevose lighthouse and gives the name and address of a nearby farm where a pony and trap could be hired to take them to the station. A telegram to the lighthouse was needed a few days beforehand for the keepers to make the necessary arrangement with the farmer.

In order to keep the story complete it should be explained that a number of off-shore lighthouses had their 'reliefs' carried out by local contractors prior to the coming of the helicopter, and not by one of the tenders. These were experienced boatmen who operated in the vicinity of the lighthouse for which they were contracted.

On the South Coast these stations were Bishop Rock, Longships, Eddystone, Beachy Head, Royal Sovereign, Hanois and Casquets, the last two being in the Channel Islands. On the East Coast there were the Longstone, Farne and Coquet but there were none on the West Coast.

However, the Wolf Rock lighthouse never had a local contractor, except for special one-off occasions in fine weather only. This was because that station was subject to such bad sea conditions for such long periods, and it was such a distance from the shore—over eight miles from the nearest point of land—that it was necessary to use the tender for every relief. It is doubtful whether any local boatman would have been prepared to enter into an agreement anyway.

Until the coming of the helicopters for the relief there was always a tender stationed at Penzance to deal with the reliefs at Wolf Rock lighthouse, the Seven Stones lightship and Round Island lighthouse. The last two were done on a regular four-weekly routine and it was quite rare for either one to suffer a delay of more than one or two days.

But for a lightkeeper on Wolf Rock a winter duty could be a nightmare. He would have to join the tender the day before the relief date and stay aboard, possibly for days, waiting for favourable weather while the tender could be engaged performing other work in more sheltered conditions. His eight-week period on duty would not start until he was actually on the lighthouse. After four weeks, halfway through his tour of duty, the next relief also might be delayed and so could the following one when he was due to be taken ashore. So his nominal eight weeks on duty could be extended three times and perhaps become twelve weeks. Some men even suffered 14 or 15 weeks in a really bad winter. Because of this the Wolf keepers were only appointed to that station for a three-year term.

Wolf Rock Lighthouse, eight miles—and occasionally fifteen weeks—from land.

Chapter 7

Life Was Not Always Dull

It might occur to some readers that the rather monastic life of the Service was devoid of humour. But human nature produces plenty of it when needed. Two good yarns I have heard concern such mundane articles as industrial rags. These are rags of any kind which have been salvaged, cleaned, sterilised and then sold for cleaning down machinery of any kind.

You can find any sort of garment in any kind of material or condition in these rags and one keeper on the Longstone lighthouse put some of them to good use. This is the lighthouse from which Grace Darling made her famous rescue mission and her bedroom was always pointed out to visitors.

Quite often some would ask if there were any souvenirs of Grace left that they could have and, quite by chance, this keeper would have a 'piece of the nightdress' she was wearing that fateful night to offer them, and no doubt he would graciously accept a suitable reward in return if it were offered. The record does not reveal how much he earned from this deceit!

The other yarn concerns the South Bishop lighthouse which lies off the Welsh coast. The keepers discovered a complete dress in one bag of rags which was found to be a good fit for the youngest keeper. The lighthouse relief was due soon after and a plan was agreed to have the young man dressed as a girl with a head scarf to complete the deception.

On the boat's approach 'she' was seen sitting alone on the rock waving a handkerchief and blowing kisses to the boat's crew! The boat's officer was said to have been on the verge of an apoplectic fit before the joke was revealed.

There was also a good rapport between all branches of the Service—lightships, lighthouses and tenders. This was not surprising, of course, since the members of all of them were regularly in each other's company during the relief trips.

One illustration of this bonhomie happened in 1950 and concerned all three branches. It occurred during a normal relief trip on the Cowes District which covered the area between Portland and Dungeness. It was long before central heating in houses was commonplace and meant that regular seafarers usually sought to leave a sufficient store of firewood for the family during their absence.

The Nab lighthouse, off the Eastern end of the Isle of Wight, frequently picked up wooden debris floating past and they had plenty of room to dry it out and chop it up to take home on the next relief day. On one occasion they managed, with the help of a dockyard tug from Portsmouth, to recover four long pieces of wooden piling, each about 15 inches square. It so happened that the keepers were keen on making door-mats from old rope if they could procure some, and the Owers lightship had plenty of that commodity after renewing the rope falls of their lifeboats.

So a deal was struck between the two stations and of course the common link between them was the relief tender, *Beacon*. The following relief day the Nab keepers asked the Captain of that ship if she could transfer a 'piece of wood' to the lightship and bring back a piece of rope. No problem he said, 'just put it in the boat when the relief is finished'.

When the 'piece' was produced it proved to be about 10 feet long and almost a ton in weight! The delivery was duly made and the exchanged rope put on board the Nab as convenient. It was all very amiable apart from the caustic comments from the Captain about 'overloading the boat' and other rude remarks from the officer-in-charge of the boat. That happened to be me so I recall the whole incident!

There was a fair bit of camaraderie and banter between the lighthouses and lightships over the radio at times. The service had its own wave band allocated for the transmission of messages to the shore via the Coastguard Service and there were two regular test calls morning and evening to check the radio equipment. After these calls it was usual for the stations to have a brief chat to each other, mainly for the purpose of reassuring any wives of station personnel who might be listening that all was well on board.

At Christmas time this became a rather illegal transmission when it was expanded into a full concert between lighthouses and lightships. This consisted of carols and sing-songs and swapping yarns and good wishes with each other which the listening families all enjoyed. I don't think this activity was ever revealed to Head Office or it would surely have been the subject of a disapproving circular from 'on high'.

When I was first married I was stationed at Great Yarmouth and the first piece of equipment I bought was a radio with the 'Trawler Band' wavelength in it. This enabled my wife to listen in at regular times while I passed information to various lightships concerning the ship's activities, particularly the expected time of the ship's arrival at the depot. Most of the other wives of the ship's company were equally pleased to hear my messages.

Some years before I joined the Service there was one unfortunate incident concerning radio messages which caused great embarrassment to the man concerned. He was a crew member on one of the East coast lightships and injured himself accidentally in the toilet by slamming the seat down behind him in a hurry and striking his very tenderest parts. The lightship master sent an urgent request by radio for the local lifeboat to take him off for medical treatment. Unfortunately the Superintendent wouldn't accept the necessity for this unless he was told the express reason for the request. As a consequence half the population of Harwich, where the man lived, knew the exact details of his distressed condition before he was even landed ashore.

In my search for anecdotes for this book I heard a number of animal stories which were a surprise to me. The lighthouse on Skokholm island for instance, had a horse called Punch. He was kept there to haul the loaded trolley from the landing place to the lighthouse on relief days, about a mile long journey. For the rest of the month he was free to wander and grazed where he wished.

On relief days it was customary to fly the Trinity House ensign at the lighthouse and from an early age Punch realised that this flag on the mast meant work for him! He would then hide away amongst the long grass and tall bushes that half covered the island. The keepers learned to be equally crafty and had to 'hobble' him two days before the relief.

One trick that Punch used to foil this was to stand in the middle of a large pond that was too deep or marshy for the keepers to wade in. Eventually the keepers learned to counter this by stretching a long rope across the pond and held by a keeper at each end. They then walked towards each other around the pond until they could finally encircle his neck and pull him out.

The island of Skokholm is overrun with rabbits and when the station was manned the keepers kept a dog who regularly ate a cooked bunny every day of its life. Also on this island is a small flock of wild sheep. They are said to be descended from some left behind by the Vikings to provide a meat supply for their visits centuries ago. This may or may not be true, but one keeper, an ex-army man, managed to kill and butcher one, to see if it was edible. It was like an old boot apparently.

I heard from three different keepers the tale of the young cockerel that was taken off to the Smalls lighthouse in late autumn one year. He was to be fattened up for Christmas and lived in a makeshift coop, with a perch, in one of the deep window recesses. This station was one of several which, in the early years, had an explosive fog signal that was set off, when needed, at five minute intervals. Each time this happened the poor bird fell off its perch. Unfortunately the station had a particularly long spell of fog, about 12 or 14 days, and the bird went right off its food and became just skin and bone.

When the fog cleared the keepers took great pains to nurse him back to good health, even feeding him with grain soaked in the Christmas brandy. But after bringing him back from death's door no one had the heart to eat him so he was taken ashore the week after Christmas and given another home.

This fog signal, a two ounce charge of Tonite, was a great nuisance to the keepers also, since the explosion would bring down a shower of soot from the flue of the coal-fired range.

On the Coquet lighthouse off the North East coast the keepers had another animal problem—a goat. This was taken off to the island as a very young kid and soon became a firm favourite. The men would nurse it on their laps, which it enjoyed of course. The trouble was that it continued to climb on them when it became fully grown. It also followed them on walks round the island, playfully butting them when they turned their backs.

Most of the keepers on these isolated stations equipped themselves with hobbies to while away their off-duty hours as the lightship crews did. All kinds of things were made: models of lighthouses of course, in wood or papier-mâché and one I saw made of thousands of match-sticks. It looked really beautiful. Plenty of budding painters tried their hand at pictures and even portraits of loved ones from photographs they took off to the station.

Several tried their hand at mat making, or knitting, and one man became so expert that he made jumpers and cardigans for family and friends, and even knitted a jersey for himself with the Trinity House crest on the front of it. Others played musical instruments, to the delight or annoyance of their fellow 'convicts'. These stone towers were often said to be worse than any prison and there were a few men over the years who had to be taken off their station when the sheer discomfort of the incarceration was more than they could endure.

One enterprising keeper on Round Island off the Scillies was a very keen gardener and spent four years constructing an excellent vegetable garden on the bare uneven rock. This island is little more than a huge rock some 120 feet high and about 600 feet at its widest part. He had first to select a sheltered hollow and build a high wall around it as protection against the gales that sweep seas right over it. He also had to bring all the soil from the mainland in sacks, mostly collected from the farmers where he lived in Cornwall. He had great help from his fellow keepers and really made a success out of his venture. He even attracted attention from the Editor of *Amateur Gardener* who gave him a three page write-up in December 1980.

Another piece of archive material that came my way is a book containing some Circular Letters issued to the Lighthouse Service pasted inside. The first one was issued in 1887 and the last in 1918 so it gives a glimpse into the lightkeepers' conditions for 31 years.

The first letter was a strict admonition regarding lightkeepers who fell asleep whilst on watch in the lantern. They were cautioned that this dereliction of duty was considered to be one of the most serious that a

Round Island lighthouse on the Isles of Scilly and the vegetable garden built by one of the keepers.

keeper could be guilty of. It would incur severe punishment consisting of being dis-rated or dismissed.

Later on, in 1896, a Supernumerary lightkeeper was dismissed for this offence after falling asleep, and for failing to report the occurrence which had been noticed, and reported, by a nearby lightship.

All lightkeepers at shore stations were required to be back on their station by one hour before sunset and in 1895 one keeper was severely reprimanded for failing to do so and was removed, at his own expense, to another station. The incident came to light due to a fire which occurred in the lantern of the station. The Principal Keeper was placed on the Pension List because there was no bucket, or flannels, in the lantern as per the written orders to deal with just such a mishap.

In 1891 the Board issued a warning about male and female children at land stations sleeping in the same room 'without due regard to decency'. The sitting room was 'to be used as a sleeping room in future if there is a large family, to remedy this state of things as far as possible.'

Annual holidays were first introduced in May 1895 when every Keeper could take 14 days leave. This was a real innovation since annual holidays for most working people were unknown at that time.

The Service regulation about not passing any information to the Press, quoted in the Preface to this book, was issued on 23rd October 1894. No indication is given regarding any special circumstance which might have given rise to the need for this caution.

In March 1899 a Circular was issued giving the daily rates of pay for Lighthouse Keepers as follows :-

Ordinary Pay—Daily Rates

Supernumerary Keepers : Unqualified	2s 6d
Supernumerary Keepers : Qualified	3s 0d
Assistant Keepers, on appointment	3s 0d
after 5 years service	3s 2d
after 10 years service	3s 4d
after 15 years service	3s 6d
Principal Keepers, on appointment	3s 9d
after 5 years service	3s 11d
after 10 years service	4s 2d

The Central Statistical Office informed me that the pound in 1900 was equivalent to £55.80p in 1998 should any reader wish to compare the above with today's wages.

There were of course benefits in the shape of constant pay, free dwellings, furniture, fuel, light, uniform clothing, medical attention, full pay while sick, pensions after 60 years service, Life Assurance and annual holidays. So it was not such a pauper existence as some might think from the low pay rates quoted above. It was interesting that every man supplied his own food at a lighthouse: each to his own can of condensed milk!

In April 1913 Trinity House issued a warning to all land lighthouses regarding Militant Suffragettes. The keepers were cautioned to exercise the greatest care when showing visitors around their station and request them to leave muffs, umbrellas and sticks in the base of the tower. It is difficult to believe that those ladies would ever contemplate damaging a lighthouse.

A typical meal at a lighthouse: one kettle for all but separate food supplies.

Referring to the issue of uniforms to all keepers, it will surprise some readers to learn that all lightkeepers wore a frock coat until 1903. In May that year Trinity House decreed that this item of uniform would no longer be supplied to Supernumerary or Assistant Keepers. No reason is given for this decision but they were continued for Principal Keepers.

Soon after World War I the Board instructed all lighthouse and light vessel personnel that they were on no account to molest any carrier pigeons that might alight at their station or in their vicinity. I suppose that until then any stray pigeon was considered 'fair game' for the pot!

There is also a warning to all keepers when cleaning the outside of the lantern glazing. This was always done from a ladder on the lantern gallery which had to be hooked on to a rail running round the outer edge of the lantern roof. Unfortunately one keeper had hooked it on to the gutter which ran round just below the lip of the roof and it was quite insecure. This was at the Longships lighthouse I believe and when it slipped the unfortunate keeper fell right down on to the rock about 110 feet below and was killed outright.

The following comic story was written in 1909 by Arthur Helliar and Cuthbert Clarke. I understand it was used by Stanley Holloway in his early years as an entertainer.

The Lighthouse Keeper's Story

You want to hear of the bravest deed ever done on land or sea?
I rather think I can tell yer that for it appears 'twas done by me.
It was when I was lighthouse keeper, a year or two back, no more.
The lighthouse was built on a rock, Sir, 'arf a mile pretty near from the shore.
A storm for a month had been raging, no boat could approach as we knew,
And the steamer wot should 'ave brought vittles was more than nine weeks overdue.
For days we'd been living on biscuits—they was all there was left to eat,
On Sundays we fried 'em in lamp oil, we did it by way of a treat.
But that give out arter a bit Sir, so we 'ad to partake of them 'rore',
Still, the lamp was the wust of the business—we couldn't light up any more.
We'd only one small box o' matches and took them above in the lamp,
And 'eld 'em afore the reflector, till my arm fairly ached with the cramp.
They didn't make much of a flare, Sir, well I 'ardly expected they would,
But I had this 'ere great consolation as I'd done all as any man could.
I soon finished up all the matches—there was nuffing more left I could do,
So I turns into me 'ammick, being sleepy, and was off in a minute or two.
Soon I dreamt that I sat at a banquet with some nobs in a West End hotel,
They was 'anding round liver and bacon, fried fish, tripe and onions as well.
A waiter asked me if I'd 'ave some, and I'd just stuck my fork in a lump,
When I almost fell out of me 'ammick, for there came a most 'orrible bump.
I knew what it was in a moment, I could tell pretty well by the force,
It was one of them big ocean liners wot 'ad got a bit out of 'er course.
There was dozens more come after that, Sir, they cannoned us all through the night,
I tell yer I wasn't 'arf glad, Sir, when I see it begin to get light.
I thought p'raps as some very likely might keep up the game all the day,
So I 'ung up a board with 'Wet Paint' on which I fancied might keep 'em away.
Being woke up all night by them vessels was enough to make anyone mad,
And the langwidge the crews used was 'orrid, and the skipper's was ten times as bad.
So I calls my mate wot was dozing, and tells 'im some oil must be got—
'There's a shop 'alf a mile off,' 'e answers, 'shall yer swim there or fly there or what?'
'I shall fly there' I says, 'or I'll try to, just 'ark while I tell you my plan,
You must fasten me on to a rocket, and aim it as straight as you can.
I must take one as well to come back with for they mightn't p'raps 'ave one on land,
But them ships knocking bits off our lighthouse is a thing as I'm hanged if I'll stand.'
So he fastened me on very careful, I'd a can in my hand for the oil,
And the wind was 'owling and screamin', and the water was all on a boil.
Now remember I says afor' startin', I'm a risking my life I'll admit,
But a Briton ne'er shrinks from 'is duty and that lamp there tonight must be lit.
Them words was scarce out of my mouth Sir, when I 'ears a loud kind of whizz,
And away thro' the air I was soaring, and a rummy sensation it is.
My mate 'e 'ad once been a gunner, and 'is aim was surprisingly true;
I missed the shop door I'll admit Sir, but bang thro' the window I flew.
But the face of the man wot was serving was the thing as you ought to 'ave seen,
When I landed full length on the counter and asks for some best paraffin.
He took me at first for a h'angel till he saw I 'adn't no wings
And notice a 'am disappearing with a loaf and some pickles and things.

To bring a long tale to a 'ead sir, I returned the same way as I came;
'Twas a coastguard as touched off the rocket, and I can't say much for 'is aim.
But my mate who was up in the tower sees me coming and 'eld out 'is net;
I'd missed by a yard if 'e 'adn't and might 'ave got 'orribly wet.
And talking o' wet, Sir, reminds me I'm dry now thro' and thro',
Wot's that you says? Will I join yer? Well thankee, don't mind if I do.
Good 'ealth Sir, its lucky I met you, for there's men 'ere by dozens as tries
To get gents to stand 'em a drink, Sir, by telling 'em 'orrible lies.

Now a museum piece, the lantern and optic from Egypt Point Lighthouse in the Solent, on the northern shore of the Isle of Wight. It has been replaced.

Electric filament lamp at Bishop Rock lighthouse—2.26 bulb, giving 1,500 watts. Both lamps beat the poet's paraffin and matches.

Chapter 8

The Steam Vessel Service

The title for the service described in this chapter was different when I joined Trinity House because it was then The Steam and Motor Vessel Service. It was changed to the one above after the war during which all the motor ships had been sunk. Now it has been changed again and is the Support Vessel Service.

Earlier in the book I mentioned my transfer in September 1940 from the East to the West Coast where a whole new chapter of experiences opened up for me. The Trinity Depot to which I was transferred at Swansea is located in the large dock system. From this depot we serviced all the buoys, lightships and island lighthouses between Milford Haven and Avonmouth. The crew were mostly Welshmen of course and recruited locally as were the other tenders around the coast.

The buoy servicing and lightship work were much the same as on the London District. But the lighthouse work was quite new to me and broadened my knowledge of the multitude of tasks which the tenders had to accomplish, mostly routine ones.

One incident worth recalling was my first experience of salvage work. This was to a ship called *Jamaica* which was loaded with possibly the last cargo of bananas to reach Britain until after the war. This occurred in late 1940 when my ship, the *Warden*, was engaged on the lightship relief which took us to the area off Newport.

We had finished working at one of the lightships and were heading for an anchorage for the night. (Ships were banned from moving after dark in that area because of the German magnetic mines being dropped.) Suddenly we saw *Jamaica* rocked by an explosion and of course headed towards her to help.

They were all ready to abandon ship when we reached her and we took them off by our boats, about thirty men I think, with only minor casualties, and the ship was left at anchor. We fully expected her to sink overnight and were surprised to find her the next day just as we had left her.

The *Jamaica's* captain of course wanted to re-board her with some of his crew and this our captain allowed him to do. But since she had been abandoned and was technically in our possession one of our officers boarded her first in order to retain the right to salvage her!

The ship's hull was not holed but her engines were found to be unusable so it was agreed to take *Jamaica* in tow to Avonmouth dock where she was bound for and already had two tugs booked. The tow went well until we were about half a mile from the dock-head and approaching the tugs to hand her over. Unfortunately our tow line parted at that point and before we could re-connect it the tugs had taken her in tow.

This meant that the tugs were not going to receive just their fee for towage but were entitled to claim for salvage since she was adrift without any engine power! I was still only an apprentice at that time so have no idea how the matter was sorted out but I did receive a share, £5, of the salvage award about 18 months later. I understood that the legal hassle about the award was further complicated by our ship having some 25 extra hands on board—the relief men for the lightships and lighthouses—and there was protracted discussion about their entitlement to a share in it.

Some weeks after this incident we had a near escape from another plane dropping mines when the ship was anchored for the night off the port of Barry. It was nearly midnight when it flew low over the anchorage area. Fortunately it was a dark night and the mine missed the target and fell outside the safe zone that our ship was in.

Early in 1941 Trinity House decided to move the oldest, and smallest, ships of the fleet to the East coast and the newest ones to the West coast. This was a sensible precaution to lessen the risk to the slightly larger ships of being mined. This plan involved my ship at Swansea being sent to the Penzance District and the one there going round to Great Yarmouth. The only thing I wasn't told was that this involved a complete change of crew except for me. I suppose nobody thought it was necessary to inform me of it.

My ship duly arrived in Penzance and moored inside the harbour. I went down to my cabin to do some study work and after a time I noticed that the ship had gone quite silent. My cabin was near the engine room and also the crew's quarters so there was often someone moving about nearby.

I went outside to see what was happening but there was no one there. Then I suddenly saw a crowd of complete strangers coming on board. They were as surprised to see me as I was to see them! They were a crew of mainly Cornishmen who lived locally and were just returning from their old ship now safely delivered to the East coast. I learnt a lot from them and we had a good rapport until I was moved again in 1943. Some of them are still alive and are still amongst my friends in Penzance.

An example of this good rapport is worth recounting. While landing stores at the Eddystone lighthouse one day with the ship at anchor I put a fishing line over the stern. Several other off-duty crew members were also there. I left my line over the side while I went to my cabin for something and on my return I had a catch on my line. I pulled it in with great excitement all round as it was apparently something big and was fighting hard to get away. But when it broke surface I found it was a frying pan which of course was skating about like a mad thing!

So began another chapter in my career because this area of the coast has very few buoy stations and only one lightship but a significant number of rock lighthouses. As I have already mentioned this was many years before helicopters were introduced to the Service and everything was delivered to the lighthouses by boat which involved hard manual labour to put all the heavy materials on to each station.

The heavy material consisted of 9 gallon wooden casks for fresh water, each weighing nearly one hundredweight, 5 gallons of oil in steel drums about one hundred pounds and sacks of coal also one hundredweight. All three commodities had to be in separate boatloads of course to avoid contamination and each boat load would total about two tons. So if the sea conditions allowed a full day's working at one lighthouse the working party would be very tired at the end of the day. This party would consist of an officer in charge, the boat's crew—at least four men—and another five or six in the shore party to assist the keepers and heave up all those stores and tip them into tanks or coal lockers.

I was very pleased to have had this insight into the special requirements of this aspect of Trinity House work. It was very useful experience when I subsequently returned to this area as the Captain of the tender nearly 25 years later.

The war was still on of course during my time as apprentice at Penzance and there were four separate incidents which are worthy of a mention here rather than in the chapter concerning wartime events.

Several weeks after my arrival in Penzance, Lord St Levan, the owner of St Michael's Mount, invited General de Gaul with his entourage and some ladies plus about 200 Free French personnel to visit the Mount one Sunday. The Officer-in-charge of some Air-Sea Rescue boats based in Newlyn was asked to supply water transport from Marazion harbour across to the Mount . He agreed to do this and produced an Operation Schedule which included the use of the Trinity ship's motor boat. There were no volunteers to take on this task on a Sunday morning of course, and two crew members, plus myself as 'boat's' officer were detailed off for it.

We were to leave Penzance at 10.00 a.m., about 30 minutes before the Air-Sea Rescue boats left Newlyn, and the final paragraph stated 'Lord St Levan's boat will be in attendance'.

When the day arrived there was a fresh wind blowing and a moderate rough sea in Penzance Bay. So of course the Air-Sea Rescue boats could not be used for fear of damage to them in the small harbour at Marazion. Our crew and motor boat were well used to such conditions and made the passage to Marazion to meet this quite large contingent of passengers.

We made our way into the entrance and fortunately the first twenty people who jumped into the boat were French seamen, looking very smart in their uniforms. The boat went astern out of the shelter of the little breakwater and almost immediately the engine failed and we were in quite a rough sea. The French men at once grabbed the oars in the boat and got us over to the harbour at the Mount while the coxswain endeavoured to re-start the engine. But his efforts were all to no avail and when we moored there we discovered that the propeller had picked up a load of thick, very strong, seaweed and we should have to wait until low water to beach the boat and clear it. So the whole operation was completed by Lord St Levan's boat which was only to be 'in attendance'.

The other three incidents all concerned the transporting of very unusual loads to, or from, the Isles of Scilly, all on separate occasions. The first cargo was highly secret and proved to be a complete radar station. This was contained in seven sealed lorries and required two trips to accomplish.

Our ships all had derricks capable of lifting 20 tons and because of our work of servicing large buoys on deck we had space on which to carry these vehicles and could lift them on and off.

The second incident was the recovery of a complete Hurricane fighter plane. The pilot had had to make an emergency landing after damage sustained in a fight and chose St Mary's Island because it had a small airfield. Unfortunately the runway was far too small to receive a fighter plane and the pilot landed without the use of his undercarriage. The plane was partly dismantled to get it down to the small quay and alongside our ship. All was successfully accomplished and we landed it in Penzance, but never heard if it was airworthy again.

The final surprising task was to take a steam-roller across to St Mary's for use there—possibly to extend the runway, although that is only conjecture. Again our lifting capability was invaluable.

This task of transporting odd loads, at no extra cost to the Service of course, was done at the discretion of the District Superintendent. I was involved with three of them during my career. Twice when I was Captain of a tender I took some heavy collecting boxes to the workshop of the Charity which owned them. These were the obsolete mine cases which one can see on many seaside promenades. They belong to the Ship Wrecked Mariners Society and regularly need an overhaul. I was also involved in organising such a load when I became a District Superintendent and it was then that I found that the source of these requests was an Elder Brother who was on the board of the Charity!

One of the outstanding memories of my time at Penzance was the sight of a wonderful display of the Northern Lights. It is very rare for them to be seen so far South and I have never heard if there has since been a display like it in Cornwall. Unfortunately it is usually a sign of bad weather coming and it was certainly the case on this occasion.

We had to leave Penzance in the early morning and anchored not far from the harbour entrance. The wind increased steadily and we were soon having a most uncomfortable time. Suddenly the anchor cable parted and we were very lucky not to have been blown on shore.

We shifted then to a more sheltered position and spent several hours lifting the spare anchor out of the hold, along with several lengths of buoy chain to form a new cable. All Trinity House ships carry a large stock of buoy chain so it was not an unusual task except that it was for our own ship's use and not for buoy work.

I obtained my Second Officer's certificate before I finished this spell at Penzance. This was another occasion when Trinity House was generous to its apprentices because during the five or six weeks I needed to study at a Nautical school in London they paid my lodging expenses, travelling costs and the school fees as well. Most other students from the Merchant Navy have to find all these expenses themselves.

That was the last significant incident I can recall while serving as Apprentice and in due course I finished my apprenticeship and was promoted to Second Officer in January 1943. This meant I was based at Harwich from where the Chief Superintendent operated.

To begin with I was an Auxiliary Officer and was moved from ship to ship wherever and whenever a need arose. There were four tenders based at Harwich by that time, so much of my service was spent hopping from one to another, with just brief spells at other depots.

This meant working with a different crew each time and another set of officers, most of whom were strangers to me. But not for long because Harwich was a busy Naval base and we were constantly involved with the many off-duty parties and dances arranged by the base for their own personnel.

Many of these were Wrens, of course, and they helped considerably to boost the quality of our leisure time. One Wren in particular was a good friend to me and we still exchange Christmas cards and news 50 years later.

More events from this period will be recorded in the chapter about our wartime activity but two humorous stories might be better told here.

There were very many Royal Navy ships at Harwich and some acted as an escort to our tenders when doing their work on the hundreds of buoys off the East Coast. On one occasion a tender was sent to attend a particularly important buoy and an escort was provided by a Frigate. It was a day of poor visibility and this escort signalled the tender to 'follow me'. After about thirty minutes the Trinity ship sent a signal to the escort: 'Your ship might be fitted with wheels but mine is not. You are heading straight for the Gunfleet sands. Suggest you follow me.'

The other story concerned a naval ship which collided with one of our buoys while entering Harwich harbour. After mooring at his berth the captain, who knew the Chief Superintendent very well, paid him a visit to report the damage. By way of a humorous touch he told the Superintendent, 'One of your buoys deliberately rammed my ship as we entered harbour'—to which the Superintendent replied, 'I'm not surprised, we have a particularly vicious type of buoy on the East Coast'.

In March 1944 I was stationed at Great Yarmouth for six years and had to adjust to another new crew. This time they were mainly Norfolk men and I was very intrigued with their interesting accent which I had not met before. Distinctly different from the Cockney, Welsh, Cornish and Essex crews with which I was familiar. During these six years I met my wife-to-be and we were married from her home in Buckinghamshire. We had a succession of homes in flats in Great Yarmouth until my next move.

During my time at Yarmouth the ship was constantly busy with buoy work and with re-establishing lightships after the war that had been withdrawn from their stations during the hostilities. This latter task was quite extended since Trinity House had lost many lightships in that time and the rebuilding programme was quite protracted. The buoy work too was much increased from the pre-war amount. This was caused by two main facets of the work. First we had been required to buoy all special 'swept channels' through our minefields, two or three hundred or more buoys on the East Coast alone. Secondly we had established about 76 new stations to mark the dangerous wrecks during the hostilities, all of which had to be serviced until no longer needed.

Neither group of extra buoy stations could be removed quickly after the war because clearing the minefields was a long and dangerous operation for the Navy, and only when that had been completed could the work of clearing the wrecks be done.

The work of attending to the buoys marking the swept channels during the war was continuous. Not only did they require routine painting and servicing, but they were constantly being damaged by ships in slow-moving convoys and also by the daily routine of the mine-sweepers which had to keep the channels clear. This was done by towing wire sweeps below sea level on each side of the sweeper seeking out moored mines, and a quarter mile long electric cable towed by the sweeper looking for magnetic mines to detonate; these lay on the sea bed. When they reached the end of their allotted area they had to swing round the buoy that was marking the channel. If the Captain did not allow enough clearance to get round then his ship would encircle our buoy with its sweep and inevitably cause damage.

After the war I counted how many times one buoy in particular, 57G, had been hit and found that seven complete buoys with their moorings had been sunk and a further 21 lanterns and seven superstructures had been swept off leaving the buoy body as a danger. The lanterns alone cost about £1,000 each to make so the total cost of this one station must have been quite enormous. There were countless numbers of similar casualties.

Some of the pre-war buoy stations in the North Sea became isolated when the British minefields were established and as a result the mooring chain of many wore out and the buoys went adrift. Some of them were picked up by our tenders if they were reported to Trinity House. Others were sunk by rifle fire from passing ships, probably because they were thought to be drifting mines. After several years of neglect they would show a lot of rust and would be floating low in the water with the weight of chain and accumulated weed and mussels, so it was an understandable assumption.

Others would actually reach the shore and be thrown up to high water mark to become embedded in the sand. Since most of our beaches were mined and out of bounds they remained there until after the end of the war.

Damaged buoy, hit by a German destroyer which lost its propeller in the collision—not surprisingly, as the buoy was made of ⅜" steel plate. The destroyer was impounded after her repairs until the German navy paid for the repair of the buoy.

In late 1946 my ship was sent to retrieve one from a beach somewhere between Chapel St Leonards and Skegness where it had lain for two or three years. It was a big one weighing about four tons and was half buried in the sand at the high water mark. A working party, with me in charge, was landed by the ship's motor boat at high tide and began to dig the sand away.

This was soon after breakfast and by the time we had cleared away enough sand to pull it on its side and roll it down to the water it was after mid-day. The tide by then had fallen enough to expose a long sand bar about 60 yards out from the beach, with a fairly deep lagoon between it and the shore. To cap it all the wind was now blowing on to the shore and had freshened up quite a bit. The captain decided to abandon the job for a better day and sent a message to the working party, about 15 men, to make their way to Skegness and we would be taken off the pier there.

We duly found our way to the road, carrying all our tools, shovels, a heavy hammer, a heavy block and tackle and a stout post. This last item was to have been driven into the sand in order to pull the buoy on to its side for rolling to the water's edge. A bus eventually arrived and the first problem was to persuade the conductor to let us on board, and I had to give a detailed explanation of why we were so dirty and of course wearing old clothes as befitted the task we had attempted, before he relented and let us on board.

On arrival at Skegness at about 3 o'clock it was then low water and the beach was dry for hundreds of yards out from the pier. We also discovered that the pier was unusable because of wartime damage, and a local boatman told us that the beach was so flat that it would be at least half tide before there would be enough depth of water to float our motor boat.

So we waited until about 8.00 pm for our boat which duly arrived. She needed to drop her anchor astern of her as the wind was quite fresh and she would require it to check her from going broadside on to the beach. But then our luck ran out because the anchor failed to hold, the boat swung broadside on to the beach and began bumping heavily. We abandoned her then and retired up the beach, wet and cold, with our numbers increased by the three members of the boat's crew, all wondering how long this ordeal would last.

Fortunately we had been seen by a policeman who knew that the wartime arrangements whereby the hotels and boarding houses co-operated to provide food and accommodation for any ship-wrecked mariners was still in force. We soon found our good Samaritan who quickly provided a meal, with some rum, and a bed for everyone in our party.

This was not quite the end of the story because I was woken up soon after 4.00 am by the same policeman who told me that our boat was high and dry, with all the boat's equipment and our tools scattered along the beach and some beachcombers were picking it over! I woke up the boat's crew and we went down to salvage the equipment and to bail out the boat. Eventually a local boatman agreed to tow her, and us, off to our ship, which was a happy ending to what had seemed like the longest 24 hours of my career.

There were two other large buoys which became beached on the Norfolk coast and have a tale to be told. It begins back in 1940 when one of our ships was mined in the Humber estuary and sank there. At the time she had several buoys on her deck which were secured by chains and bottle screws. This was standard practice, to ensure they did not slide across the deck if the ship was rolling, as they could easily kill or maim someone. Some of them weighed five tons or more.

When the ship sank all those buoys went down with her and remained chained on the deck for several years. Eventually the action of the sea broke the chains and set the buoys adrift. Two of them reached the East Coast, one in the mouth of the Wash and, by astonishing luck, the other one reached Great Yarmouth and became beached about 200 yards from the harbour entrance. It was from this port that it had begun its journey on the ship's deck and was considered to be the most intelligent buoy we had, since it obviously knew its own way home!

It had to remain on the beach for several years until it was considered safe to walk there, when it was finally dragged off by one of the tenders and carried to the depot. It was still perfectly usable after some chipping and painting. Plenty of the Trinity House buoys have given more than a century of service.

When my time at Great Yarmouth came to an end my next move was to the ship at Cowes in November 1950, and I had promotion to Chief Officer as well. In the Merchant Navy this rank is called 'The Mate'. By this time Trinity House had increased the ships complement of Officers to include a Third Officer, much to our relief. The ship there was called the *Beacon*.

My move meant more house hunting, of course, while my wife waited at Yarmouth. There were plenty of houses on the Isle of Wight to choose from and, after she had been down to vet it, we bought our first real home just outside Cowes.

I now had another crew, many of whom I knew, but as with all the Trinity House tenders the majority of them were long serving members and were well used to 'breaking in' new officers to their particular routine! The buoy and lightship work was just the same as on the East Coast but now I was again involved in lighthouse work.

These stations were Beachy Head, near Eastbourne, and the Hanois and Casquets, both in the Channel Islands. We only did the relief at Beachy Head, since the other two reliefs were looked after by local contractors, but we were often required to take over pieces of equipment or heavy stores that the contractors could not handle. In addition, we had several buoy stations to attend to.

It was nearly 20 years before the Beachy Head relief was taken over by a contractor and this was concurrent with the removal of the Royal Sovereign lightship and the establishment of the Royal Sovereign light tower in its place. This will be explained later in the book.

There were two other lighthouses in the Channel Islands whose reliefs were done by men living locally, but the work of refurbishing all four stations following the German occupations was then under way after much of their machinery had been remade, and thereby hangs a tale!

One of these items was a complete new optic for the lantern of the Casquets lighthouse. This is a very large item and was delivered to the ship at Southampton (to save the cost of transport to the Isle of Wight) and was beautifully crated up in about 50 or 60 different sections, many of which were quite large. Unfortunately there was no Delivery Note, so we had no idea of the contents of each crate, only the number painted on each one.

We duly arrived at the Casquets and began unloading the crates under my supervision. This was my first visit to the station so I had no prior

Beachy Head lighthouse.

knowledge of the optic or of the landing operation. This latter was by ship's motor boat and the crates were lifted out by a block and tackle fixed to a crane post. (The actual crane had long since disappeared.) This lighthouse was built nearly three centuries ago on the top of a small rocky island and the only way up is a long pathway hewn out of the rock.

Only a very few of the cases could be carried up and the larger ones went up 'end over end'. A most tedious job it was. While this was going on I walked up to the lighthouse dwelling and was met by a man in white overalls. He turned out to be the engineer sent out by the makers of the new optic to erect it and he produced the missing delivery note which he had brought with him. By then quite a number of the crates had reached the lighthouse courtyard and he asked me, 'Which one has the mirror in it?' That was the very first moment that I learned that this lighthouse was to have a concave mirror, 26 inches in diameter, behind the light source and my heart nearly stopped.

The crate was quickly identified and opened up to expose the shattered remains of that beautiful mirror. It was fortunate that I was there at the opening because it was quickly apparent why this disaster had happened. The mirror was mounted in a square frame to hold it rigid when put in position, and this frame in turn was mounted in a larger one and held by adjustable screws. This arrangement was to allow the mirror to be finely adjusted to bring its centre exactly horizontal with the centre of the light source.

Alas, the man who packed it had not secured the two frames together and the mirror had been rocking backwards and forwards on the journey from factory to lighthouse. We just stood in stunned silence looking at this disaster. In addition, this crate had not been placed inside a larger crate and cushioned by rubber against shocks in transit. There was a spare mirror fortunately and when we opened that crate the contrast in packing arrangements was astonishing. This one did not need the two steel frames since it was a spare, and was packed in a special, polished, box with a sorbo rubber bed for storage in the lighthouse. That case had itself been packed in a larger crate and was cushioned all round by rubber. After my report went to Trinity House I never heard another word about the matter, although I have no doubt it was raised with the manufacturer!

Casquets Lighthouse: the tower on the right, marked H, now has a helicopter pad on it.

Having now reached the status of a 'senior officer' I was allowed to practise handling the ship ready to take charge when the Captain went on leave or perhaps went ashore as acting-Superintendent.

This led to my second experience of salvage work which arose during one of those occasions. This was to a Pilot Cutter belonging to Trinity House which was disabled near Ryde. My ship was sent out to assist her and we ended up by securing her alongside our ship in dense fog, taking her back to Cowes and putting her into dry-dock there. There was no salvage award for this little episode but it was all good experience.

Bardsey.

Just over three years later I found myself on the move again, this time to the Argus stationed at Holyhead. This meant selling up the house at Cowes and buying again at the new station, a process which took nearly seven months to accomplish. There was no help from Trinity House with the actual house-hunting and purchase and sale of property, but at least there was an allowance for the disturbance under the Civil Service rules.

The transfer to Wales was another new experience because the ship was nearly new and was much bigger than almost any others that Trinity House had built. It was a replacement for one of those lost in the war. Most of the crew were Welsh and spoke Welsh all the time, but they were all bilingual so there was no difficulty in communication on the ship.

One interesting thing I remember about this crew is that they had a proper team of soccer players and also a cricket team. Officers were included as well—there is no distinction of rank on a sports field! These teams had been in operation for many years and had regular fixtures, not just at Holyhead but at several ports on the Holyhead District which extended from Fleetwood to Milford Haven. When the ship was engaged on routine buoy work it was quite easy for the Captain to arrange his programme of work to allow for a night anchorage at the Isle of Man, Barmouth, Aberdovey and elsewhere on the coast. Prior to leaving her depot a quick telephone call was all that was needed. Other ships in the Trinity House fleet also had such teams but I never heard of them having any similar away games around their respective districts.

The Island of Bardsey which lies off Aberdaron had a very alarming incident which involved the keepers of the lighthouse there. The seeds of this were sown during my time on the Holyhead district although it was all unknown to me at the time. This island is large enough to support a farm and there are a number of other houses which are used by holiday-makers.

In June 1955 a young Polish man called Jan by some and known by others as Bert Panek, came to live in one of these houses and very quickly became a recluse. He said he had come for peace and meditation and was very religious. By 1958 he had a long beard, straggling hair and seemed to be tormented in his mind. It was very worrying for the few people living on the island.

Eventually he became quite demented and had to be constrained by one of the light keepers, Harold Taylor, who, fortunately, had been a policeman. An urgent message was sent by the keepers for medical help. The *Argus*, then in Holyhead was despatched at midnight with two police officers on board who brought a straitjacket with them. Jan was then sent to a mental hospital and recovered in time. The whole episode can be found in Brenda Chamberlain's book *Tiderace*.

The Holyhead District stretched as far south as Milford Haven which was a very useful 'safe anchorage' for our ship on occasions. Near the inner end of the Haven one of the earliest Trinity depots was established at Burton, near Neyland. It is still there, much dilapidated, but still recognisable as having been built by Trinity House. It was discontinued when the present depot at Swansea was built in 1925.

My stay at Holyhead was only three years and I was transferred in 1957 to *Patricia*, the flag ship of the Service at Harwich. I had had previous short spells of duty on her so I was familiar with the ship. She was quite a unique one in some respects: she was built in 1937 and was one of the few diesel-electric ships that Trinity House ever had. She also had extra accommodation for the use of Elder Brethren when she was used for their annual inspections of all the buoys, lightships and lighthouses around our coasts.

She also has the unique honour of leading the British Monarch whenever he or she is afloat in our territorial waters. This happens once or twice during the year and is a privilege greatly cherished by all in the Service. I had the pleasure of being on board on several of these occasions before being moved to other ships stationed at Harwich. There were four of them at that time and these transfers all helped to broaden one's knowledge and experience.

Eventually I was the senior Chief Officer and was designated 'auxiliary'. This meant I was no longer attached to one ship but was 'on call' to relieve Captains of any ship during periods of leave or sickness.

On one of these occasions in 1963 I had a most unique task to perform. Trinity House were considering the possibility of replacing some lightships with light towers. One proposed site was at the eastern end of the Varne Bank which is a sandbank off Folkestone. The first consideration was to have the sea bottom beneath the bank investigated by taking core samples on the proposed site. The *Ready* was given the task while I happened to be acting as her captain and a small drilling rig was mounted on her fore-deck. We had to moor the ship for two weeks over the selected position in such a manner that she could not move more than six feet in any direction, apart from an up-and-down movement as the tide rose and fell. This was to ensure that the drilling tube hanging over the side, and sunk into the sand, would not be dislodged or broken.

There were quite a few doubting Thomases in the depot who said that it could not be done, but by using some heavy mooring buoys borrowed from the Admiralty with four-ton anchors we managed the task. We even survived a day of gale force wind although we had to suspend drilling that day. Otherwise drilling continued day and night and the work was completed in ten days instead of the estimated fourteen. The cores showed that the underlying sea-bed was not suitable for 'planting' a fixed tower and the lightship remained on station.

Later on, in 1971, I was involved in establishing one of these towers. It was not purpose built as a light tower but had previously been a very big drilling platform built for the National Coal Board in the 1950s. It was to enable them to calculate the extent of the massive coal reserves which lie under the North Sea just off the Northumberland coast. It was designed to be placed on the sea-bed for a core to be taken from the coal seams hundreds of metres down and then to be lifted and moved from site to site. It was a laborious job, but a successful one. The tower had plenty of accommodation under the top deck so was suitable for conversion to a lighthouse, and consequently it was bought by Trinity House.

The work was done in Hartlepool dock where it dominated the skyline for two years since it was over 200 feet high. When at sea it was moved between two large barges, purpose-made for the job, and towed by two tugs. Both barges had two powerful electric winches with two very strong wires, to lift the tower off the bottom and high enough to secure the base of it tight under the bottom of each. It was a most cumbersome thing but it did work successfully for a number of years.

When the conversion work was almost completed Trinity House decided to put a marine officer in charge of the actual move from

Former Trinity House flagship, *Patricia*. She was sold out of the service about 16 years ago and became a floating restaurant in a Swedish harbour.

(photo: Alfred H. Smith)

Inner Dowsing tower after alteration, waiting to be towed to her station off the Wash in 1971.

Hartlepool to a position well outside The Wash. There it took the place and the name of a lightship called the *Inner Dowsing*. I was then captain of *Stella* at Penzance and was temporarily detached from my ship for two months and sent to oversee the voyage which fortunately was successful.

Inner Dowsing tower en route to her station.

This tower lasted until 1994 when it suffered damage by a ship colliding with it. The tower was then removed and replaced by an automatic lightship. The method of removal was by use of a very huge floating crane called 'Noble Lifter' with a 400-foot jib. This crane simply plucked the 650-ton lighthouse from its position and carried it to Lowestoft to be scrapped.

Earlier in this chapter I mentioned the Royal Sovereign tower which replaced a lightship of that name off Eastbourne and this operation was in progress at the same time as that of the Inner Dowsing. It was a much more extensive project than the one with which I was involved. The tower was built mostly of reinforced concrete and the base was hollow. The work was done on a beach site not far from Newhaven harbour. It was therefore a purpose built lighthouse and not a conversion as the Inner Dowsing was.

Inner Dowsing tower removed, without ceremony, by a giant floating crane in 1994. It was taken to Lowestoft to be scrapped.

This tower was built in a huge depression dug in the shingle deep enough to float the tower when a channel had been opened up to flood it. Tugs then towed her to the position of the lightship where the hollow base was then flooded and the tower grounded. This base was afterwards filled with sand and gravel to make sure it stayed in position.

Returning to my career, It was some time after my involvement with the Varne Bank boring job that I was given my 'brass hat' and became captain of *The Vestal* in 1965. She was a sister ship to the Ready and Argus who were all built after the war, and she was stationed at Harwich. During my time on this ship I had two incidents which I have never forgotten.

In July 1965 we were sent to the Channel Islands to attend to some buoy work there. While proceeding down the English Channel we ran into dense fog off Beachy Head and shortly afterwards, about midnight, we heard an S O S message from Niton radio station to say that a collision had occurred. A Greek ship named *Nymfea* had been struck by a Liberian ship called *Francesca*. She was manned by a German crew. We answered the distress call and were able to locate both ships on our radar quite quickly and proceeded to the scene.

After 40 minutes we found a lifeboat with fourteen people in it from the Greek ship, some of whom were injured. The injuries were caused when the lifeboat had capsized on launching. We then lifted the boat on to our foredeck to prevent it being a hazard to other ships and put the survivors in the officers' lounge, where first aid was administered where needed.

Soon afterwards we spotted another boat on the radar which we also picked up. It was a lifeboat belonging to the *Francesca* and had been launched by her Captain to look for possible survivors from *Nymfea*. This boat was now lost in the fog and two miles from her own ship, so we left it hanging over the side ready to be sent back to *Francesca*. There were six men in it and they also were shown to the Officers' lounge which soon turned out to be a grave mistake. As soon as the Greek survivors realised that this new influx of 'survivors' were in fact part of the crew of the ship that had rammed them, a serious confrontation began which my officers had to stop. Very soon after this we located the two ships on radar and, after getting *Francesca* to identify herself by blowing the whistle, because it was still dense fog, we sent the German crew back to her.

On close approach to *Nymfea* we found that the remainder of her crew—eight men—were abandoning their ship into a second lifeboat alongside her. Only the Captain and two officers remained on board. Our motor boat was then sent across with one officer and as soon as this boat reached *Nymfea* those eight men promptly scrambled into it. This meant a return trip to get them on board *Vestal* before my Second Officer could get on board *Nymfea*, assess the situation and then, on my instructions via his portable radio, offer her captain a tow to a position of safety.

Her captain accepted this offer under the terms of Lloyds Open Agreement. This is a No-Cure, No-Pay Agreement drawn up by Lloyds Underwriters and is legally binding even if only made by word of mouth. *Nymfea* could not communicate by radio because her aerials had collapsed when the collision occurred. She was very badly damaged on her port side near the stern and her plating was ripped open right down to the bottom of her hold. The impact had embedded the Liberian ship's anchor in her plating and then it had broken the shaft off. The head of the anchor remained there until eventually she went into dry dock.

I decided to tow *Nymfea* to the shelter of the Solent, the nearest suitable place. We disconnected one of her anchors from its cable, connected our five-inch towing wire to it and paid out about 75 fathoms of her cable to act as a 'spring' while we were towing. *Nymfea* was lying with her stern almost level with the sea and her bow well out of the water and towering above us. This meant that the work of connecting up the tow was exceptionally hard since it all had to be done by hand. My comment at the time was that we looked like a puppy pulling an elephant!

As we were about to start towing, the Eastbourne lifeboat appeared out of the fog and I was able to pass the survivors over to her. This was not without an understandable reluctance on the part of the survivors, which we managed to overcome by lowering their suitcases and kitbags into the lifeboat so that they had to follow.

Greek ship *Nymfea* aground on the Ryde Middle Sand in the Solent after being salvaged by *T.H.V. Vestal* with the help of German tug *Hermes*. The *Vestal* is on the far side of the casualty with her funnel and her stern just visible. The *Hermes* is attempting to pump water from *Nymfea* in spite of the massive hole in her side which reached from her deck to her keel.

Here you see how much of *Nymfea's* bow was out of the water, with her stern firmly aground. The harbour authorities boat has now joined the party!

The hole in *Nymfea's* side made by the *Francesca*. It almost reached down to the casualty's keel. Note the portion of *Francesca's* anchor still embedded in the casualty's side. *Nymfea* was pictured here in dry dock awaiting repair.

A view from inside the casualty, showing the broken anchor. It was securely lashed by now to stop it falling out.

Soon after the tow started a German salvage tug named *Hermes* appeared out of the fog to my great surprise, and offered to take over the tow or assist us. She had never once called on the radio to offer help before this although clearly she had been monitoring all the radio messages.

I could not refuse this assistance because under the rules governing salvage one is required to take every measure possible to ensure the safety of the casualty. If I had failed to get her to safety after refusing the tug's help I could have been sued by her owners and possibly even prosecuted. There was the added complication in this case that the Greek captain would have nothing to do with the German tug since his ship had been damaged by another German-crewed ship. However, I accepted the tug's offer on my own behalf and not *Nymfea's* and entered into a sub-contract with the tug's owners.

Eventually we reached the Solent and grounded the casualty on a sand-bank after approval from the Southampton Harbour Master and Salvage Association officials. We did this because she was riding at such an acute angle, bow out of the water and her stern awash, that I knew she would never be able to enter dry dock like that. In addition I considered that she might take in more water—enough to sink her—if she was not grounded and perhaps had to wait several days to be put on an even keel.

I then dismissed the tug—quite a difficult task I might add—and arranged for the English salvage firm of Risdon Beazley to take over the task of putting the casualty on a more even keel and then into a Southampton dry dock for repair. They had a lot of work to do beforehand to patch the hole and pump her out.

After this episode, which lasted three days, we were able to continue our journey to the Channel Islands. The salvage award was made 18 months later and amounted to £28,000. It was of course shared and the apportionment was £13,000 to Risdon Beazley, £10,000 to the tug, £1,000 to myself and £4,000 to the crew of *Vestal*.

The other episode happened in November of the same year and was nearly a disaster. We were detailed to tow one of the lightships from Harwich to the Tyne for a routine dry-docking. It should have been a routine trip as well until the weather turned bad and we had to take shelter in Grimsby Roads.

After two days at anchor (the lightship had her own anchor down too,) the Master told me she was running out of coal for the galley fire. The bunker had been nearly empty when we left Harwich as it had some repairs needed and there was only enough for the trip to the Tyne. There were six men in her towing crew.

I decided to go into Grimsby Dock for the night to pick up a ton of coal for the lightship which remained at anchor. On the way into the dock we had a collision with a fish carrier. She was flying the flag 'G' which is the international signal meaning 'I require a pilot', so I had assumed she was just waiting to go to sea.

Nothing of the sort though, she had a pilot on board, having come in from sea and the flag had been forgotten. The result was that when the dock gate was opened for us to enter the other ship thought it was for her and turned across our bow. She sustained quite a lot of damage as a result and went into the dock ahead of us. She turned out to have been converted for use as a Geophysical Survey craft in the search for oil in the North Sea. This involves dropping small charges of dynamite and recording the shock waves through the sea bed. I learned afterwards that she was carrying two tons of dynamite in her hold which was stowed at almost the exact point of collision! She was not flying the flag 'B' either, which is the international signal meaning 'I am carrying explosives'.

After leaving Grimsby we resumed towing the lightship but had another mishap when we encountered a gale and our towing wire parted in the night. The lightship dropped her own four-ton anchor so was soon secure enough for us to leave her and seek shelter for ourselves. The tow was resumed after two days waiting for the weather to improve and we finally handed the lightship over to the tugs at Tynemouth. We then returned to Harwich after what seemed the longest trip of my life.

Some years after *Vestal's* salvage job the *Patricia* had a similar task in the North Sea in February 1974. She heard a distress message from a German roll-on, roll-off ferry named *Leila* that she was aground on a sand bank off Haisboro in Norfolk. She had received damage to her bottom plating as a result and all the cooling water intakes for her machinery were blocked with sand.

Patricia successfully pulled her off the sand bank intending to anchor her to await the arrival of a salvage tug. But no one answered the call so *Patricia*'s captain entered into a No-cure No-pay agreement with *Leila*'s captain to tow her to the Humber.

It proved to be a very difficult task because *Leila* had no power to pull *Patricia*'s towing wire on board except by hand, which was not practicable, and two ropes had to be used. Because of bad weather later in the passage to the Humber the ropes parted and they had a difficult time reconnecting the tow to *Leila*.

Eventually she was safely berthed in Immingham and *Patricia* could continue with her work. The salvage award was £12,000.

The following year, in August 1966, I was transferred to Penzance to take charge of the *Stella*. Yet another sudden change in my station as mentioned previously. Once again I was house hunting while waiting to sell the one I had had built only two years before. It was a difficult time for my family which now comprised my wife and two young schoolgirls.

The girls had not moved home since they were babies so it was quite upsetting for them to be suddenly confronted with the news of being moved to some mysterious place 'at the end of the world' and losing all their friends at Harwich.

Trinity House tender *Vestal* towing the Outer Gabbard light vessel to her station after a refit.

Stella returning from buoy work with the evidence of her efforts on the foredeck.

However, they all coped very well when they all moved in the following January and the girls soon settled into new schools and new recreations. In fact one eventually married while I was stationed there and we now have two Cornish grandchildren.

Shortly after the family moved down, I had three unpleasant incidents in quick succession. First my mother died in Wiltshire and while returning from her funeral I heard the news of the *Torrey Canyon* disaster on my radio. This gave my ship the task of removing most of her crew, while the local lifeboat stood by to take off the remainder if required. Subsequently we had to remove the Seven Stones lightship while the wreck was bombed to set the oil alight and then took her back to her station.

The third incident happened when I was acting as District Superintendent a few weeks later while he was on leave. The Chief

Stella effecting relief at Seven Stones. She is moored to the stern of the lightship, while delivering fresh water via the hosepipe from her bow. (photo: Norman Fitkin)

Officer, who was an old friend of mine, became acting Captain but while the ship was engaged on buoy work at Plymouth he had a massive heart attack while he was actually manoeuvring the ship and fell dead on the Bridge across the engine telegraphs.

In spite of this rather sombre start to life in Cornwall it turned out to be the most enjoyable of all the places where I was stationed. I thoroughly enjoyed working with the Cornish crew and taking the ship in and out of the small harbour. I always said she was like a big fish in a small pond, since she was the largest ship that ever went regularly in and out of the dock. There were other slightly larger ships that occasionally put into Penzance but none did so on a regular basis.

There were several incidents worthy of a mention while I was at Penzance. This was several years before helicopters were introduced and the ship still serviced the rock lighthouses by sending fresh water in barrels and oil in drums to be manhandled from boat to tower. I decided to experiment with mooring the ship close enough to their landings to be able to run hoses ashore to enable us to pump direct from the ship's tanks.

Each of the five stations, Bishop Rock, Round Island, Wolf, Longships and Eddystone had been closely surveyed by the Hydrographic Service many years ago. Large scale charts had then been issued for each place and we had copies on the ship. All of them showed deep water quite close to all the various landings, so by a process of trial and error we found the best places to anchor fairly near to each one, only in fine weather of course.

Having got the ship settled with 60 or 70 fathoms of cable out and lying to her anchor we used the motor boat to run a rope away to the lighthouse landing. When this was secure we hove the ship closer to the landing so that she was nicely held between anchor and lighthouse and could not sheer about on the tide. We then ran an oil and a water hose ashore and let the pumps do the rest. My only regret is that I did not think of taking any photographs of this operation, although I do have several taken by a lighthouse keeper at the Bishop Rock. Since they were taken from the tower they do not show ship and lighthouse on one exposure.

Stella moored to the base of Bishop Rock Lighthouse. Her Port anchor is down to ensure that she does not get too close to the tower.

Stella's hawser secured to Bishop Rock Lighthouse. It completely circles the base of the tower and is secured by a steel bar. As soon as this is removed the rope drops free.

This was not the first occasion that such an operation was performed as someone did a similar thing at the Wolf some years before World War II but he was so severely criticised by his Superintendent that it was never done again. However, the reason given by the Superintendent was that he should have been attending to some other work elsewhere instead of the Wolf's needs.

Sometime in November 1969 we had a very interesting and quite prestigious service to perform. Admiral Sir Michael Le Fanu had recently been appointed as First Sea Lord at the Ministry of Defence and he decided he did not know enough about the Trinity House Service and requested to have a working trip on one of the tenders.

The choice fell on *Stella* at Penzance and it was arranged that we should land him on the Wolf lighthouse and also the Seven Stones lightship. We duly cleaned the ship of course and welcomed him on board early one morning with his A D C and a party of press photographers. Unfortunately it was a very stormy day and there were no prospects of landing him on the Wolf but there was just a chance that we could put him on the lightship. Captain D A G Dickens, one of the Elder Brethren, was also in the party. Sir Michael could only spend that one day with us so we duly took passage. It turned out to be a really awful trip and all the press people were seasick, but the Admiral really enjoyed it. He had no previous experience of a lighthouse tender and was very impressed with the ship's performance.

On arrival at the lightship the sea was almost too rough to put the boat down but having brought him out there we did not want to disappoint him and he duly made his visit. None of the press men were fit to go with him and only one or two even came on deck to see the operation. Later on, during the return trip, he was taken off by helicopter from Culdrose air station.

Sir Michael really enjoyed his trip and was impressed with our boat work in rough sea conditions. He was good enough to write to me on his return to the M O D and his letter read as follows :-

> It's only when one does an outing like Friday's that one realises how little one has known about so much for so long. Of course, over the years I have read a great deal about your Service but just a few hours with you taught me more than all that reading.
>
> I was tremendously impressed by the cheerfulness and professionalism everywhere apparent—particularly perhaps in the way you handled your ship, your boat's crew handled their boat, and your stewards handled the soup.
>
> Thank you very much for everything and for your very kind and generous hospitality.
>
> Yours sincerely
> M Le Fanu

Later on in my time at Penzance we had another small salvage job. This happened on a day that we were landing stores at the Longships. It was a fine day but quite windy so that the sea was quite rough for small ships passing round Lands End. As we finished the job and began to leave someone noticed a small tug having a poor time and a man on the bridge waving frantically.

We sent our boat away to see what her problem was and found that she had been rolling heavily enough to ship water, which had stopped her engine and she was drifting ashore and required a tow. We duly offered our help and towed her round to Penzance. This service earned us a reward of £250 from her owner which all on board shared of course. The name of the tug was *Hooligan* which gave us all a good laugh.

Soon after this incident I had another period of 'detached duty' from my ship. Trinity House had begun planning the reduction of their fleet of nine ships and the eventual introduction of helicopters, both of which were the subject of rumours throughout the Service but nothing else. Eventually I learned that Trinity House were considering a scheme called 'double manning' for their fleet and wanted a serving officer to help them get the scheme running. The choice fell on me and I spent five weeks in London at the Headquarters working on the details.

Quite simply, the plan was to halve the fleet and have two separate and complete crews on the ships they retained. It involved quite a lot of planning and various calculations about the estimated savings to Trinity House. But it was well worth it because it was arranged that each crew would serve 14 days continuously on the ship followed by 14 days liberty. This was a vast improvement to their conditions of service since they were certain of having two weeks at home out of every four.

Admiral Le Fanu on Seven Stones light vessel—wih no pressmen in evidence. Sir Michael and Capt. Dickens have just finished a tour of the light vessel.

Admiral Le Fanu leaves Seven Stones light vessel after his inspection. He is half-way down the ladder and Capt. Dickens is at the top of it.

Previously we had all been 'on call' between each trip at sea except for 14 days annual leave. The savings to Trinity House arose from the fact that the most expensive 'tools' they had, their ships which cost six or seven million pounds each, were now utilised throughout the year with no idle time. It was an accountant's dream arrangement! They only needed to return to base every fortnight for stores, food and other provisions, and to change over the crews. This changeover day is always on a Wednesday.

As a 'fore-runner' for this new arrangement Trinity House had introduced Centralised Catering for all their ships in 1970. This was known as Company Feeding in the Merchant Service. A Catering Manager was appointed and he had a department at Harwich Depot which dealt with the four tenders there, ordering and supplying food for all on board. The ships at the outlying depots were also his responsibility and were supplied by arrangements with local catering companies. It was welcomed by all crews since it meant that not only did they feed very much better but it also amounted to a pay rise since Trinity House paid all the costs. It was all part of the enormous changes beginning to take place in the Service.

The outcome of all this was that four ships were sold off and one was retained as a reserve to replace any of the remaining four which needed an overhaul or was laid up for any other reason—breakdown or damage perhaps. This scheme took several years to come to fruition, in easy stages, and most of the crews were very pleased with it since they now had 14 days guaranteed off duty time in return for 14 days at sea in theory. They actually had only 13 days free in fact, since most of them had to travel some distance on the Wednesdays, but that was really unavoidable. The midweek changeover was to ensure that the depots were fully manned and to avoid weekend travel.

Sadly it did not suit everyone though. The Service has always had a few men on each of their ships who were single and quite content to live permanently on their ship, considering it as their home. Now they had to vacate their 'home' every fortnight and live in digs. They also had to clear their cabin each time to let some complete stranger take it over. We lost quite a number of reliable men as an unforeseen result.

The use of helicopters was starting about the same time and this meant that Trinity House now had only five ships to be equipped with a helipad on their stern, which was another saving.

Since that rather hectic period change has continued in the Service and now there are only two ships to cover all the coast of England and Wales. This further reduction in the fleet has been brought about by new technology leading to the automating of all lightships and the rock lighthouses, plus a huge reduction in the work required to maintain the buoyage around our coasts. The buoys still remain on station but they now have lanterns powered by solar panels which charge batteries lasting at least four years. In addition, the buoy bodies are now painted with epoxy resin paint which also lasts for four years and they do not require to be painted annually as before.

Some time after my detached duty at Trinity House I was transferred once again, back to Harwich to become Captain of the *Patricia*. This appointment turned out to be for only one year due to an unexpected retirement, but I enjoyed being in command of a ship that I had already served on in three different capacities. During that year I was actively involved in the change to 'double manning'. It had originally been thought that this could not be applied to *Patricia* because of her special duties. These were her occasional escort of *H M S Britannia* when she carried Her Majesty the Queen, and her other task of taking the various inspecting Committees around our coast. However, it was quickly realised that all the four ships would have to be double manned or none at all and I was busy with arranging her first itinerary under the new scheme.

This meant that planning her schedule for each Committee trip had to allow for a 24 hour visit to a different port every fortnight and always on a Wednesday. It may sound complicated but it was not too difficult and the same arrangements made then, in 1973, still hold good today.

Each of the two crews on the ships is a complete unit, from Captain to galley boy. At first some of the senior personnel, accustomed to being responsible for everything in their particular department, found it difficult to hand over to their 'opposite number', but all of them quickly settled down and the system still works well after nearly 25 years.

I finally left the sea-going part of my career in 1974 when I was promoted to Assistant Superintendent at the Harwich office and worked closely with the Chief Superintendent there. The double manning of the tenders involved the meticulous advance planning of each ship's programme, starting on a Wednesday, for the whole fortnight. Previously the programmes had been quite relaxed, just a discussion between the Superintendent and the Captain at the start of a week. Now the double manning scheme meant that the Captain joined his ship on the Wednesday with a prepared programme waiting for him and he was expected to sail soon after. If that programme involved buoy work, taking clean buoys to sea or perhaps overhauling a lightship's cable, the shore staff had to be instructed well in advance to have the necessary items ready to load. All this forward planning had to be done by the Superintendent concerned.

One other great advantage of double manning for officers and men alike was that everyone could live where he wished, within reason. He no longer had to shift his home and family on transfer to another station but simply had to be willing to travel to and from his home for the change-over day. This did mean that some crews had a long journey from Penzance or Holyhead to Harwich or Swansea but it was considered 'the luck of the draw'.

The reduction of the fleet had another effect that not everyone had foreseen. It meant that the number of depots could be decreased, together with the posts of District Superintendent. Trinity House then altered the boundaries of the various Districts in 1974 so that only three remained, the East, West and South Coasts. The Superintendents involved all retired in due course and those posts were not filled at Holyhead, Penzance and Great Yarmouth.

After four years at Harwich I received my final promotion. This was to District Superintendent of the South Coast district based at Cowes. It was another move of course but with the consolation of having the promotion to go with it. The District stretched from Dover right round to the Trevose Head lighthouse near Padstow on the west coast and included the Channel Islands stations, quite a large 'parish'.

There was no ship attached to the depot as the four tenders were divided between bases at Harwich or Swansea. Whenever one was needed on the South coast it was arranged in co-operation with the Superintendents at East or West. Now there are only two tenders, one each at Swansea and Harwich, and only one Superintendent, at Harwich.

I remained at Cowes for six years and enjoyed it very much. It included a good deal of travelling to carry out regular inspections of the lighthouses and the lightships. The era of helicopter use was now getting into full swing so I was able to make good use of their services. We could not arrange for one to be available for our exclusive use but it was quite simple to tailor one's need to fit in with the relief programme every fortnight.

Eventually, in 1983, when I had reached the age of 60 I decided to retire. I had then served 44 years with Trinity House and felt it was time to step aside for a younger man to put a foot on the promotion ladder. Sadly this did not happen because my post at Cowes was very soon abolished in the shrinkage of the Service.

In the first chapter I put a complimentary couplet about the Elder Brethren, but it was part of a longer poem which may be a fitting end to this chapter.

> Deny ourselves and work for others, is the creed of Elder Brothers.
> Superintendents bear the brunt and have to face both back and front.
> Captains vary quite a lot, some are human some are not.
> Nothing disturbs the Engineers if you'll let them sleep and stand them beers.
> When the lightship Master writes his log he fiddles up the hours of fog.
> But the life of a lamplighter when afloat, comprises duties quite remote.
> He trims his lamps, then mixes 'duff'—
> I think by now you've heard enough.

Chapter 9

Wartime

This chapter, devoted to describing the wartime activities of the Corporation of Trinity House, has to commence several hundred years ago to give a true picture. People are often surprised at the length of time that the Corporation has existed, which is mainly because Trinity House has never been keen on advertising itself and certainly not during wartime years.

The first involvement in warlike activities was during the Dutch invasion of the River Medway in 1667. Their ships managed to reach Chatham and did a great deal of damage there. There was a fear that their next action would be an invasion of the Thames and an attack on London. Trinity House were asked to provide a blockage in Gallions Reach on the Thames and they scuttled several ships there on the 13th June 1667.

The Brethren were also asked to take control of the shore batteries at Gravesend but fortunately the invasion scare did not materialise and presumably Trinity House also had the task of removing the blockships.

The next warlike occasion was the Mutiny at the Nore which began in May 1797 with Richard Parker as the leader. It was quickly realised in London that the fleet would be likely to defect to the enemy—either Holland or France—and arrangements were put in hand by Trinity House, in conjunction with the Admiralty, to have all the buoys and beacons in the Thames estuary destroyed. This job was mostly done under cover of darkness and was completed by the 8th June, and several of the Elder Brethren took part in the operation by sailing with the small craft employed.

When the mutineers learned what was being done by Trinity House they threatened to hang any of the Elder Brethren that they caught. Shortly afterwards they did capture one, Captain Calvert, and dragged him on board the flagship for a drumhead court martial. He managed to persuade them that their cause was lost and because of his brave manner he was released unharmed.

The next warlike operation by Trinity House was caused by the threat of Napoleon's possible invasion of London in 1803. The Board's proposal to counter this possibility was to commission and equip 10 frigates, at Trinity House expense, carrying from 28 to 40 guns each and to moor them across Lower Hope Reach in the Thames. Each ship had 60 men on board and they were commanded by Elder and Younger Brethren. Some Naval commanders were appointed to assume overall control of this fleet.

The Muster Sheets for these crews still exist and show a very mixed bag of men variously described as Seamen, Landsmen, Volunteers, Pilots, Lascars, Harbour Volunteers, Marines, River Fencibles, Greenwich Pensioners, East India Company Pensioners, about 1200 in all. Which might indicate that not all survived the full term of their engagement.

All the cost of this enterprise was borne by Trinity House and the frigates remained on guard until late in 1805. The total cost was about £10,000, an immense sum, and the enterprise was called the Royal Trinity House Volunteer Artillery. When I first visited Trinity House in my apprenticeship days there were several stained glass windows in the Board Room commemorating this event, but I do not know if they all survived the blitz in London or not.

It appears that the years between that event and World War I were devoid of warlike activities, but that situation changed abruptly in 1914. I am able to list some of the major operations carried out by Trinity House, which will indicate to the reader just how busy the Service was in those four years.

There were 51 lightships on station around our shores at the outbreak of the First World War and twenty of those on the East coast were withdrawn while eighteen remained on station there with lights extinguished. Twenty-four temporary lightship stations were established at various times, each one requiring an immense effort to equip, overhaul, tow to its station and to be maintained there. A steam ship named 'Argo' was temporarily fitted with a lightship's mast and lantern to mark the position of the Sunk station and was then instructed to shift her position frequently to mislead enemy submarines.

Four principal beacons in the Thames estuary were cut down to water level to prevent their use by the enemy. 205 new buoy stations on the East coast were established to mark the 'swept channel', while most of the original peacetime buoy stations were removed.

Thirty lighthouse lights were extinguished but the stations were kept manned so that a light could be shown for Fleet movements. Various small lights were established on the coast for Admiralty purposes. For instance, many wrecks had to be located and buoyed if necessary.

Regrettably, two of the ships were sunk by mines with inevitable loss of life. The Roll of Honour for 1914—1918 shows the names of 6 Headquarters staff, 5 lighthouse staff, 18 lightship staff, 37 steam vessel staff and 30 from the Pilot Vessel Service. Some of these men would no doubt have been volunteers in the Armed Forces.

The Service was also called upon to lay special buoys for naval operations as far afield as the White Sea, Persian Gulf, Sierra Leone and Malta. This job was done by specially commissioned Merchant ships adapted for the job and carrying some Trinity House personnel to oversee and direct the operation. One of them, the *Wirrall* was torpedoed off the Norwegian coast with the loss of all the buoy equipment but no loss of life fortunately.

After the end of World War I a huge operation was mounted to bring back the several million Prisoners of War from the camps in Europe. It was necessary to have a distinctive 'swept channel' from Calais to Dover to ensure the safety of all the ships required. Trinity House decided to do this by laying a line of five lightships in 1919 and a Circular Letter calling for volunteers to man them was sent out which I feel sure was fully answered.

During World War II the involvement of the Service was equally protracted and even more expensive than in 1914—1918. It included the loss of four ships from the fleet of nine, with heavy loss of life on two of them. All these four losses were caused by enemy mines, two in the Thames estuary—the *Argus* and *Strathearn*; one in the mouth of the Humber—the *Reculver*; and the *Alert* while working off Arromanches soon after D-Day. In the case of the *Argus* there was only one survivor out of 34 men. *Strathearn* lost half of her complement and many of her survivors were unfit for further service at sea afterwards.

As in World War I the workload increased dramatically from the onset of war, beginning with the laying of very many lighted buoys to mark the 'swept channels' along the east and southeast coasts. There were three tenders at Harwich and one each at Blackwall and Great Yarmouth which were all quickly involved. Soon afterwards the tenders at Cowes and Penzance were also brought to the East coast for several weeks to help with this task.

The work also involved the extinguishing of some buoy lights in the Thames estuary and the fitting of dimming screens to many others. All this was in addition to the usual maintenance required and the regular relief work on lightships and lighthouses.

In spite of that 'phoney war' epithet invented by the media the sinking of Allied and neutral ships began from day one. The *Athenia* was actually sunk by a submarine off the north coast of Scotland in the dark hours of 3rd September 1939. This was quickly followed by mine-laying activities both by Britain and Germany. Fortunately for us some sharp-eyed look-out on the coast of the Thames estuary spotted one of the magnetic mines floating down on a parachute one night on to the Shoebury Sands and recorded it accurately enough to enable the boffins to find it at low water. They eventually managed to de-fuse it and find how we could counteract the deadly things.

As already described, I was witness to one large Japanese passenger ship being mined, but there were many other victims along the East coast. Only three days before the *Terukuni Maru* went down another large passenger ship, *Simon Bolivar*, was also sunk in the same vicinity with the loss of over 80 lives, and there were many more around the same time.

All these wrecks meant added work for Trinity House ships to find and mark them. We also had to keep a sharp look-out for drifting mines of the horned variety. These were laid outside our territorial waters by ourselves as well as the Germans and they quite often broke adrift in stormy conditions. We were supplied with old Lee Enfield .303 rifles to

Trinity House vessel *Reculver*, sunk in the mouth of the Humber.

(photo: P. A. Vicary)

enable us to sink them if possible and this could be quite a hazardous task. Under the Geneva Convention these moored mines were required to have a device to render them inoperative when they broke adrift, but for a variety of reasons it did not always work. I remember that on two occasions our target exploded and sent bits of shrapnel flying on board.

Trinity House itself became a casualty when the blitz on London began. It was totally destroyed by incendiaries on the night of 29th January 1940. Much of their archives and valuable relics had fortunately been sent to safety outside London, but one large furniture van full of valuable paintings was left outside the building prior to despatch into the country next day, and everything in it was destroyed.

Captain P. E. Goodman shooting at mines. Apprentice Tarrant looks on.

(photo: *Sea Breezes*)

Yarmouth depot, heavily damaged in the war.

Another casualty was the Trinity depot at Great Yarmouth which was partly destroyed in an air raid in 1941. The *Alert* was berthed there at the time and her crew helped to fight the blaze until the ship had to be shifted to a safer berth. There was the usual store of acetylene cylinders for the buoys at the depot and the ship's crew removed these from the burning store at considerable risk to their safety.

Quite early in the war our ships were being attacked by enemy aircraft. The first one was *Reculver* in January 1940 which was hit by a bomb and machine gun bullets while on a lightship relief trip. The Second Officer was killed and over 50 others were injured. The ship was immobilised and had to be towed into port. She was later towed to London for repair in the East India dock.

My own ship, the *Alert*, was first attacked on 25th July 1940 by three fighter bombers off Dover. The bombs all missed but came very close, and their bullets wounded several men on board. Luckily I was not among them! By that time our ships were beginning to get an occasional

Wartime damage to Trinity ship *Reculver* by German aircraft off the Norfolk coast in 1940.

Reculver in the East India dock, awaiting repair.

escort vessel and I remember on one trip early in 1940 we had the Polish destroyer *Grom* looking after us. She was the biggest destroyer afloat at that time and almost new.

Trinity House remembered the loss of two ships sustained in the last war and were soon actively seeking replacements in anticipation of needing them. After the fall of France the Service acquired two French buoy laying ships that had reached Plymouth safely and these were re-commissioned and used by us until the end of the war. In addition Trinity House purchased a deep sea trawler and converted her for use as a lightship relief ship and for towing. She was not able to lift buoys but was a very useful addition to our small fleet, and remained in service until 1960. Her name was *Triton*.

Trinity House vessel *Triton*.

The French ships were called *Andre Blondell* and *George de Joly* and had a large crane on their fore-deck for buoy work, unlike the conventional derrick that our ships had. These ships were returned to France after the war. They were built in 1929 and the *George de Joly* was still working in 1993.

Trinity House also acquired another ship as a temporary war-time replacement. She was the research ship *Discovery II* and was loaned by the Ministry of War Transport in early 1941 until the war ended. By that time the swept route for shipping had extended to the Farne Islands and this considerably increased the work load since it also had to be marked by our buoys.

Fortunately there were no other ship losses until the *Alert* was mined off Arromanches, but the air attacks on our ships continued relentlessly, and there had been almost 30 when the war finished. Early in the war our ships had been armed with 12-pounder guns on their sterns and various sorts of machine guns which no doubt deterred some of the planes from pressing home their attacks.

The *Satellite* had one particularly unpleasant experience before she was transferred to the East coast in 1941. She was attacked with bombs and bullets for nearly 30 minutes somewhere off Land's End and one bullet hit a container of cordite on the after deck and set it on fire. This cordite was the propellant for the shells used in her 12-pounder gun and was in a heavy steel box on her stern. Fortunately the gunner saw it in time and with the assistance of the ship's boatswain they threw it overboard to explode about thirty yards astern of the ship. Both men received the Lloyds medal for Gallantry at Sea as a result.

All our ships had two of these Navy gunners from the DEMS section, which stood for Defensive Equipped Merchant Ships.

When the war started all the tenders were at once painted grey all over, as were most Merchant Navy ships. A few months later Trinity House instructed us to paint 'LIGHTHOUSE SERVICE' in two foot yellow letters along each side, but they had no deterrent effect on the enemy and were painted out three or four months later.

We also laid a number of buoys in foreign waters as was done in World War I. This happened after Denmark was overrun and as a result Iceland was occupied by the Allies until the war ended. The Admiralty was required to set up a naval base near Reykjavik and *Patricia* was sent to buoy the approach channel to it. A second trip was made by the *Discovery II* a year or two later to service and check them all.

Satellite suffered another air attack some time in 1942, by a Dornier aircraft, which gave her a few moments of 'glory'. They successfully fought off the plane and the incident was later reported by the BBC as being the only hostile activity on our coast that day. But Lord Haw-haw's interpretation of the event was 'the successful sinking of a 14,000 ton naval transport by the gallant Luftwaffe'.

In 1940 *Alert* witnessed much of the Dunkirk evacuation, but we were not permitted to take part. The Admiralty forbade this because our ships and their trained crews were considered too valuable and indispensable to be risked. *Patricia* did get caught up at the start of the operation because she was sent to lay some buoys to mark a safe 'swept channel' across the Dover Straits and was shelled by the enemy but was not damaged.

After the fall of France, long-range guns were sited on her coast by the Germans who were then able to shell any ships seen in the Dover Straits and Dover Harbour. Several of our ships and unmanned lightships became targets for the gunners although none received a hit as far as I know. Probably this was because there were very few ship movements in daylight at that time. If our ships had to attend one of the lightships or a damaged buoy they were given a naval vessel to lay a smoke-screen around the position.

The lightships themselves were frequent targets for the enemy aircraft and many were hit by bullets and several were sunk by bombs with loss of life. The first attack was at the end of January 1940 on the East Dudgeon lightship well out from the Lincolnshire coast and was badly damaged although she did not sink. All seven of her crew and a mechanic who was working on board abandoned her in one lifeboat. After rowing all night in bitterly cold weather, they reached the coast near Skegness but were overturned on the beach by the sea and seven of them were drowned. The one survivor eventually recovered and transferred to the tender stationed at Yarmouth.

'Incidents' reported in the press were not always what they seemed, however. The picture on page 115 with its original caption 'attack in

Satellite in more peaceful times. Built between the wars, she spent most of her life as the working ship between Lyme Bay and the Isles of Scilly.

progress' is a glaring example of misinformation. It is a perfectly normal relief operation for one of the light vessels marking the Goodwin Sands.

ATTACK IN PROGRESS—THE CREW ABANDON SHIP

A relief operation made sensational by the press.

The bombed Goodwin Lightship beached at Deal. This was an example of German disregard for the neutrality of lightships.

Nevertheless, as mentioned in the chapter on lightships, almost twenty of them were lost during the war. Fortunately most of them were unmanned, but at least two of them were still manned and everyone on both were killed. These losses ocurred in the North Sea and the Thames Estuary.

Lighthouses too were targets for enemy planes and the St Catherines station on the Isle of Wight lost all three keepers in one raid. They were all in the engine room one morning when it received a direct hit by a sneak raider on 1st June 1943. Fortunately none of the dwellings were damaged and all the keepers' families survived without injury.

In August 1941 the Longstone lighthouse off the Northumberland coast was bombed and suffered severe damage but there were no deaths. The repair of the damage had to wait until 1952, I believe. The Wolf Rock lighthouse was shot-up by an enemy plane in 1941 and the lantern glazing and the optic inside were severely damaged, but no injuries were caused to the keepers.

Early in the war when the Channel Islands were about to be occupied one of our ships, the *Vestal*, was sent urgently to evacuate the lighthouse keepers from the four stations that were under Trinity House ownership. It was a hazardous task but accomplished safely and without any casualties. The ship had been the first *Patricia* and used as the Committee ship until 1938. She still had the extra accommodation that had been used by the Elder Brethren which was very fortunate since she also brought back nearly 100 refugees from the islands.

St Anthony lighthouse at the entrance to Falmouth Harbour had a lucky escape in March 1941 when a land mine was dropped on the cliff top above it, without any damage or casualties to the station. The *Smalls* keepers also had a nasty fright when they observed a mine bobbing about in the landing gut near the lighthouse. A message to the Superintendent at Holyhead invoked the instruction to 'take no action to clear it and open all windows in the tower'. Nothing else is recorded so presumably the hideous thing found its own way out.

The *Beacon* carried out a surprise rescue in January 1945. She was anchored in Yarmouth Roads during a strong North Easterly gale when the look-out spotted two men on the Scroby Sands waving. Thinking of airmen who had ditched, Captain Harris sent the motor boat over to investigate and it returned with two Germans from a midget submarine that had run aground on the sandbank. They blew it up before getting into the *Beacon's* boat and were subsequently landed by an RAF rescue boat bound for Yarmouth.

From early in the war all our ships on the East coast were supplied with a small barrage balloon as a defence against low flying aircraft. They were a great comfort to the personnel on board, of course, despite the extra task of taking them on and off the ship when leaving or entering port. The ships were all fitted with a small winch on the deck carrying enough wire to fly the balloon several hundred feet up.

Later on *Beacon* carried out another rescue, in the Dover Straits this time, when we were engaged on buoy work somewhere to the east of the Goodwin Sands. This was the day of the raid on Arnhem which went so tragically wrong. During that morning we were witness to the huge fleet of gliders and their tugs passing over us and saw quite a number which were in difficulties and had to ditch in the Channel. There were several rescue craft stationed out there against this possibility but one came down close enough for us to send our motor boat across before it sank. It was a cargo carrier with two jeeps on board and four American personnel. They were very wary about our boat at first and had revolvers at the ready in case we were Germans. Goodness knows where they thought they had ditched, for the white cliffs of Dover were still in sight! Later on we transferred them to one of the rescue boats for passage to the shore.

Another incident in the Dover Straits was experienced by the North Goodwin lightship. This was early in 1945 shortly after she had been re-laid on her station towards the end of hostilities. Her crew were somewhat startled to hear a foreign voice on their radio after dark which they nicknamed 'luscious custard', They could not understand the brief message he sent but it was repeated several times on consecutive nights. Eventually the call-sign was deciphered as 'Ludwig Gustave' and was finally identified by a naval ship as a midget submarine which would surface after dark to transmit a message. The naval ship was able to deal with it quite effectively.

As could be expected, Trinity House ships were actively engaged in the D-Day operations. Before any details were known all Merchant Navy personnel were canvassed to ask for volunteers to take part in any warlike operation. As far as I know all Trinity House seafarers did so and we all had the letter 'V' marked on our identity cards.

Preparations for this historic event entailed the stock-piling of dozens of buoys and their moorings at the Cowes depot, which took many weeks to complete. These had to be assembled, fitted with acetylene cylinders and their lanterns, painted and identified with their station number, and finally stored in 20 large Thames barges in the River Medina. Three small Admiralty tugs were on loan for this work, which took many weeks to complete.

The final event was the arrival, two weeks before D-Day, of six of the Trinity House ships which were to be the work-horses to put all this equipment on station. They were *Patricia*, *Discovery II*, *Alert*, *Warden* and the two French ships. They loaded their first consignment of buoys and waited for the word to go. Their first task would be to lay 73 buoys at pre-arranged positions and there was a final conference with the Admiral in charge, at Portsmouth, with his officers, the Trinity House Superintendent and the six Captains of the Trinity ships.

This meeting apparently started with an element of farce about it when the senior Naval officers objected to the Trinity House personnel being fully informed about the locations of the landing areas on the French coast. This was finally resolved when it was pointed out by the Superintendent that he would have to be given the positions that the buoys were to be laid in so it would be quite obvious to all concerned in the operation what the landing areas would be!

The first task on D-Day was given to the two French ships, *Andre Blondell* and *Georges de Joly*, and they were required to follow behind the mine sweepers soon after nightfall laying small temporary, lighted buoys to show the swept channels. The other four ships followed a little later with the standard six-ton buoys which took much longer to lay. The work of all six ships to and fro between the Cowes depot and the French coast was continuous until all the stations were established.

Several weeks after the operation started two lightships were laid by our ships off the French coast and they were fully manned by our personnel. They were also armed defensively with machine guns but I do not believe either of them were attacked. One was called *Kansas* and marked the route into Cherbourg and the other was *Juno* and marked the approach to the Mulberry harbour.

Every time our ships returned to Cowes they had to be refuelled, water tanks filled and food supplied, in addition to loading replacement equipment, buoys, chains, sinkers and so on. The fuel and water were

Trinity House Lightvessel *Juno* and the tender *Warden* off the Normandy coast, June 1944.

(from the painting by Rowland Langmaid, by kind permission of the Elder Brethren, Trinity House, London)

supplied from special tankers which also tended on all the other ships used in the invasion fleet, landing craft, tugs and naval ships. In addition to establishing those first new buoy stations our ships had a continuous task of renewing or repairing those which were sunk or damaged. The immense amount of traffic using those swept channels resulted in many casualties to those buoys and in the first four months there were 350 damaged or sunk by collision.

As the Allied advance continued into France and Belgium so our ships advanced with them, marking the new swept channels that were required and also the numerous wrecks along the coast.

Prior to this advance eastward the *Alert* had been mined not far from the Mulberry harbour and sank quite quickly. Fortunately there was no loss of life and the crew were picked up by the *Patricia* which was following behind her. Both *Vestal* and *Patricia* were involved in collisions during this period and suffered quite serious damage to their bows, but managed to get back to England for repairs. The *Vestal* had not been part of the initial task force since she was required to attend to the usual Service work along the South coast. This was also the task of the other ships of the Trinity House fleet, *Beacon* on the West coast,

Satellite and *Triton* on the East. I was on the *Satellite* at the time and have clear memories of the almost continuous round of attending to buoy casualties.

It was during this period that the V1 rockets (doodle bugs) started and we were witness to the first one coming over near Dover *en route* for London. Some very muddled reports of this filtered through to our base at Great Yarmouth before our return. It resulted in a bizarre story going round the town that we had been damaged and casualties received. On our return a few days later, one of the crew called at his local on his way home and discovered a collecting box on the counter for his 'widow'. It may be amusing now, but it was an unnecessary shock for his family.

A fuller account of this whole episode in Trinity House history is to be found in Woodman's book *Keepers of the Sea*, but I do not know of any other complete account of our participation in that momentous period of British history. We did receive copies of a letter to Trinity House, congratulating all concerned on the work performed, from Admiral Ramsey who was the Allied Naval Commander-in-Chief of the Expeditionary Force. It is reproduced at the back of the book.

All the wrecks in the waters under the Trinity House jurisdiction remained their responsibility under the Merchant Shipping Act of 1894, but it was plainly impossible for us to undertake the task of clearing them. As a result the Admiralty Wreck Dispersal Department was set up in June 1941. This was due, in the first instance, to the many wrecks blocking the inshore channels and some port entrances. Captain Gerald Curteis an Elder Brother, later Sir Gerald, was seconded from Trinity House to be the Director of Wreck Dispersal and work was started promptly. In spite of their efforts, when the war finished there were 428 wrecks remaining to be dealt with and the department had to continue the dispersal work until 1958 when the responsibility reverted to Trinity House. Admiralty control of shipping also had to be continued for several years until all the mines were cleared, along with many of the wrecks.

The Roll of Honour for 1939 to 1945 shows another long list of names, beginning with the Master of Trinity House himself. He was the Duke of Kent and was shot down while on active service with the Royal

Another reminder of wartime dangers: anti-aircraft gun at Casquets Lighthouse, left behind by the Germans, who had occupied all the Channel Islands.

Air Force only a few months after he was selected to be Master. Following him are the names of one Elder Brother, two Younger Brothers and four of the Headquarters staff. Then come the names of four lighthouse staff, 27 lightship staff, 51 Steam Vessel staff, three depot staff and 17 from the Pilot Vessel Service.

In wartime as in peacetime, those who worked in the service of Trinity House faced great dangers and provided an invaluable service to others. This account of the history of the service is written in tribute to them all.

Captain Michael Tarrant at Cowes Trinity House depot, on his last day of service.

Appendix: Letters in recognition of war efforts.

C O P Y
Allied Naval Commander-in-Chief
Expeditionary Forces
c/o Admiralty
LONDON
S.W.1

3rd September 1944

DEPUTY MASTER, TRINITY HOUSE

1. I wish to place on record my high appreciation of the invaluable work performed by the vessels of TRINITY HOUSE and their crews, as well as by those who have been responsible for the organisation and preparations ashore, during recent operations involving the landing on the Continent of Europe of the greatest sea-borne expedition in History. The great success achieved was due in no small part to the contribution of TRINITY HOUSE.

3. Success is seldom achieved without loss, and it was with great regret that I learnt of the loss of T H V ALERT on the 16th June. She had done fine work close off the enemy coast and it was most gratifying to know that none of her crew was lost.

4. I shall be grateful if you will convey my appreciation to all of TRINITY HOUSE.

(Sgd.) B H RAMSEY

ADMIRAL
ALLIED NAVAL COMMANDER-IN-CHIEF
EXPEDITIONARY FORCE

C O P Y

TRINITY HOUSE, LONDON, E C 3

10th October, 1946

Est. 2480/1946

The Superintendent,
East Cowes.

1. With reference to your letter of the 26th ultimo, submitting reports relative to the loss of the anchor and mooring wire belonging to the S S 'Barndale' in a position near the Shambles Light Vessel on 24th ultimo and the attempted recovery thereof by grappling operations during which it was found that a magnetic mine was attached to the cable, the Elder Brethren have ordered that the acting Master, Mr C F HORN, and the other personnel concerned in the hazardous task of paying out the wire and lowering the mine to the sea bed viz:- MR P D JONES, Temporary Second Officer (acting as First Officer), Mr E J GASH, Temporary Second Engineer, and C F FORD, Boatswain, be commended for the parts taken by them in this operation.

2. Please communicate the foregoing to the personnel concerned accordingly.

(sd) J M NICOLLE